THE WORK OF THE FUTURE

THE WORK OF
THE FUTURE

BUILDING BETTER JOBS IN AN AGE OF
INTELLIGENT MACHINES

DAVID AUTOR, DAVID A. MINDELL, AND
ELISABETH B. REYNOLDS

FOREWORD BY ROBERT M. SOLOW

THE MIT PRESS   CAMBRIDGE, MASSACHUSETTS   LONDON, ENGLAND

This book was set in Stone Serif and Avenir by Jen Jackowitz. Printed and bound in the United States of America.

Library of Congress Cataloging-in-Publication Data

Names: Autor, David H., author. | Mindell, David A., author. | Reynolds, Elisabeth B., author. | Solow, Robert M., writer of foreword. | Massachusetts Institute of Technology. Task Force on the Work of the Future, issuing body.
Title: The work of the future : building better jobs in an age of intelligent machines / David Autor, David A. Mindell, Elisabeth B. Reynolds ; foreword by Robert M. Solow.
Description: Cambridge, Massachusetts : The MIT Press, [2021] | Includes bibliographical references and index.
Identifiers: LCCN 2021010583 | ISBN 9780262046367 (hardcover)
Subjects: LCSH: Employees—Effect of technological innovations on—United States. | Technological innovations—Social aspects—United States. | Automation—Social aspects—United States. | Labor market—United States. | Income distribution—United States. | Technological innovations—Government policy—United States. | Labor policy—United States.
Classification: LCC HD6331.2.US A98 2021 | DDC 331.250973—dc23
LC record available at https://lccn.loc.gov/2021010583

10 9 8 7 6 5 4 3 2 1

CONTENTS

FOREWORD

Robert M. Solow[*]

I am writing this in the last week of January 2021. Sixty years ago, almost to the day, my family arrived in Washington, DC, and I started a year's work on the staff of President Kennedy's Council of Economic Advisors. The US economy had not yet emerged from the "typical postwar recession" of 1960. The unemployment rate, as I remember it, was a hair under 7 percent.

But another, more difficult problem had arisen. Each of the last three typical postwar recessions had taken place at higher unemployment rates than the ones before. Some economists and many in Congress and the financial press were suggesting that this higher unemployment rate was not the usual sort. It reflected not a lack of demand for goods and services but the fact that the unemployed workers were unqualified for employment: they were in the wrong place or had the wrong skills or no skills at all, or inadequate education. The usual fiscal and monetary policy maneuvers would do no good at all.

There is a tendency, whenever there is unexpectedly high or persistent unemployment, for simple monocausal explanations to circulate. Blaming the unemployment rate on the characteristics of the unemployed is

* Robert Solow is Emeritus Professor of Economics, MIT. He won the Nobel Memorial Prize in Economics in 1987.

one such. There is a certain immediate plausibility to such an explanation. The unemployed do tend to be less qualified than the employed. But whatever the true source of the unemployment, the normal process of turnover and selection will eventually focus the unemployment on the least qualified. This certainly does not mean that training the untrained will increase employment.

Here is a simple analogy: think of a high school basketball game played in a gym with a fixed number of seats bolted to the floor. Tickets are free, and more spectators arrive than there are seats. The seats will go on the average to the quick and aggressive. For the slow and passive there is standing room. Now suppose you train the standees to be faster and more aggressive. At next week's game more of them will get seats. But the total number of seats does not change at all. Getting employed in a modern industrial economy is a lot more complicated than getting a seat at a basketball game, but you see the point.

This was an important matter when the Council of Economic Advisors tried to calculate appropriate fiscal and monetary policy. My first assignment from Walter Heller, the council chairman, was to evaluate this theory of rising "structural" unemployment. This being Washington and not MIT, I think I had three weeks. My conclusion was that there was certainly an element of structural unemployment but there was no evidence that it was increasing.

Of course, blaming the characteristics of the unemployed is not the only simplistic way to account for unexpectedly high and persistent unemployment. Dramatic changes in technology are another and equally common theory. I first heard the word "automation" during that 1961 debate. We are already beginning to hear that the robots are coming, the robots are coming (and some day they will actually come).

The current situation is different. Leaving the COVID-19 pandemic aside, there has been no long-run rise in the unemployment rate, at least not yet. What we have instead is something more complex.

For generations, the real wage rate in the US had grown at more or less the same rate as output per hour of work. This meant that their ratio, the share of output paid out in wages and salaries, had no trend. There were short-run variations but not much else. That seems to have changed in late 1960s or early 1970s. The real wage trend began to fall short of the productivity trend. It was not that the productivity trend accelerated; that might suggest something technological going on. The difference was that real wages fell behind. That involves a lot of economics, especially when it is set beside David Autor's famous finding that the economy was providing lots of low-wage and high-wage jobs but was losing the middle-skilled employment that had been part of the American Dream. The dramatic increase in inequality of income and wealth fits in here, too.

Now there were many candidate causes, and they were not mutually exclusive. Those middle-skilled jobs may have been lost to workers in poor, low-wage countries. Workers were clearly losing bargaining power, as evidenced by the virtual disappearance of labor unions from the private sector. Employers hardened their attitudes. The general market power of large firms in concentrated industries was probably increasing, maybe by a lot. The problem was not to pick a cause but to reckon how much weight to attach to each of a list of causes, and that is a very hard thing to do. It follows, of course, that fitting remedies to the disease, if it is a disease, is equally complicated.

By the way, I do not want to leave the impression that education and training are minor factors in all this. Certainly maintaining a skilled and adaptable labor force makes a necessary contribution to productivity. Second, easy access to education can function as an equalizing factor, although it is pretty clear that it does not perform this function very well in the US. Finally, the system of education and training maintains a common culture and a common understanding of citizenship. The point I was making just now was only that more training or even better training does not necessarily lead to higher employment.

During the first seventy years or so of the twentieth century, American capitalism pretty regularly delivered about three-fourths of the national income in the form of wages and salaries. That is the trendless number I mentioned earlier. During the past forty years or so that number began to diminish, and it had reached something like two-thirds when the pandemic arrived. That is still much the larger part of national income. At that scale, any major change in the labor market is bound to have consequences for the rest of the economy, consequences that will then reflect back on the labor market. Disturbances arriving from outside the labor market will directly influence outcomes in the labor market. That is why, instead of being a dreary recycling of the work skills needed for oncoming technologies, this book turned into a wide-ranging survey of the economy as it now appears. No doubt we will need another such report someday, perhaps when the robots arrive. In the meanwhile, read on and learn what the grown-ups are thinking.

1

INTRODUCTION

A decade ago, powerful mobile phones were still a novelty, driverless cars were never seen on public roadways, computers did not listen to conversations or respond to spoken questions. The possibility of robots taking jobs seemed far off, save for an assembly line or two. But as the emerging capabilities of robotics and artificial intelligence (AI) began capturing headlines and the popular imagination, researchers and commentators began warning that jobs long thought to be immune to automation—those demanding expertise, judgment, creativity, and seasoned experience—might soon be better accomplished by machines. Citizens of industrialized countries took notice, reacting with mounting trepidation.

In this context, in the spring of 2018 MIT president L. Rafael Reif commissioned the MIT Task Force on the Work of the Future. He tasked the group with understanding the relationships between emerging technologies and work, to help shape public discourse around realistic expectations of technology, and to explore strategies that might enable a future of shared prosperity. The Task Force was co-chaired by this book's authors, Professors David Autor and David Mindell and Executive Director Dr. Elisabeth Reynolds. Its members included more than twenty faculty members drawn from twelve departments at MIT and more than twenty graduate students. The Task Force commissioned and conducted numerous research studies, many of them published as working papers and research briefs, on which we draw heavily for this book (a complete list of Task Force publications is presented at the end of the book).

In the three years that the Task Force delved into the future of work, autonomous vehicles, robotics, and AI advanced remarkably. But the world was not turned on its head by automation, nor was the labor market. Despite massive private investment, technology deadlines have been pushed back, part of the normal evolution of breathless promises as concepts are tested in pilot trials, integrated into business plans, and actualized in early deployments. These are the diligent, if prosaic, steps toward making real technologies work in real settings to meet the demands of hard-nosed customers and managers.

Our research did not confirm the dystopian vision of robots ushering workers off factory floors or AI rendering superfluous human expertise and judgment. But it did uncover something equally pernicious: amid a technological ecosystem delivering rising productivity and an economy generating plenty of jobs (at least until the COVID-19 crisis), we found a labor market in which the fruits are so unequally distributed, so skewed toward the top, that the majority of workers have tasted only a tiny morsel of a vast harvest.

For most US workers, the trajectory of productivity growth diverged from the trajectory of wage growth four decades ago. This decoupling had baleful economic and social consequences: low-paid, insecure jobs held by non-college-educated workers; low participation rates in the labor force; weak upward mobility across generations; and festering racial earnings and employment disparities that have not substantially improved in decades. While new technologies have contributed to these poor results, these outcomes were not an inevitable consequence of technological change, or of globalization, or of market forces. Similar pressures from digitalization and globalization affected most industrialized countries, yet their labor markets fared better.

Yet we know that history and economics show no intrinsic conflict among technological change, full employment, and rising earnings. The dynamic interplay among task automation, innovation, and new work creation, while always disruptive, is a primary wellspring of rising productivity. Innovation improves the quantity, quality, and variety of work that a worker can accomplish in a given time. This rising productivity, in turn, enables improving living standards and the flourishing of human endeavors. Indeed, in what should be a virtuous cycle, rising productivity provides society with the resources to invest in those whose livelihoods are disrupted by the changing structure of work.

When innovation fails to drive opportunity, however, it generates a fear of the future: the suspicion that technological progress will make the country wealthier while threatening numerous livelihoods. This fear exacts a high price: political and regional divisions, distrust of institutions, and mistrust of innovation itself. This anxiety has been laid bare in US politics as a growing gulf between the "haves" and the "have-nots" has driven a deepening national schism over how society should respond to the needs of those at the bottom of the economic ladder.

The central challenge ahead—indeed, the work of the future—is to advance labor market opportunity to meet, complement, and shape technological innovation. This drive will require innovating in our labor market institutions by modernizing the laws, policies, norms, organizations, and enterprises that set the "rules of the game."

The labor market impacts of technologies like AI and robotics are taking years to unfold. But we have no time to spare in preparing for them. If those technologies are deployed in the labor institutions of today, which were designed for the last century, we will see similar effects to recent decades: downward pressure on wages and benefits and an increasingly bifurcated labor market.

This book suggests a better alternative: building a future of work that harvests the dividends of rapidly advancing automation and ever more powerful computers to deliver opportunity and economic security for workers. To do that, we must foster institutional innovations that complement technological change.

We are living in a period of significant disruption, but not of the kind envisioned in 2018, when the Task Force was launched. The final phases of researching and writing this book occurred during the 2020 months of COVID-19, when citizens of many countries were in a state of pandemic lockdown. Our technologies have been instrumental in enabling us to adapt to these new circumstances via telepresence, online services, remote schooling, and telemedicine. These tools for performing work remotely don't look anything like robots, but they too are forms of automation, displacing vulnerable workers from low-paying service jobs in such industries as food service, cleaning, and hospitality. We face a labor market crisis stemming from the COVID-19 pandemic. Millions are unemployed. But technological advances did not cause this crisis.

Long before this disruption, our research on the work of the future made it clear how many in our country are failing to thrive in a labor market that generates plenty of jobs but little economic security. The effects of the pandemic have made it even more viscerally and publicly clear: despite their official designation as "essential," most low-paid workers cannot effectively do their jobs through computing platforms since they must be physically present to earn their livings.

Some forecast that robots will soon take over those roles, though few have to date. Others see the indispensable role of human flexibility since it is human, not machine, adaptability that has allowed us to reorganize work on the fly during the pandemic. Still others see COVID-19 as an automation-forcing event—a catalytic force that will pull technologies from the future into the present as we learn to deploy machines in jobs that humans cannot safely perform. However it plays out, the effects of COVID-19 on technology and work will last long beyond the pandemic, although those effects may look quite unlike what anyone envisioned in 2018.

Other forces have also roiled the 2018 visions of the future, including the rupture between the world's two largest economies and a surge of political turmoil and economic populism that culminated in a violent attack on the US Capitol in the wake of the 2020 election of President Joe Biden. These pressures are reshaping alliances, breaking apart and reorganizing global business relationships, and spurring new forms of cyberwarfare, including disinformation, industrial-scale espionage, and electronic compromising of critical infrastructure. The US and China had friction before, but nothing like the fracture that is now occurring. What began as a trade war has morphed into a technology war. China's whole-of-government approach to tackling major industrial and technological goals poses a competitive challenge for Western economies, which typically take a decentralized, often business-led approach. It remains to be seen whether China's focus on government-driven domination of data accumulation yields technological advances beyond creating powerful tools for monitoring and controlling its own population.

The clash with China is rippling through the economy and threatens to hinder innovation, which increasingly emerges from countries around the world, often by researchers who are collaborating across borders and time zones. How can we make sure that technological advances, whenever they come, yield prosperity that is widely shared? How can the US and its workers continue to play a leading role in inventing and shaping the technologies and reaping the benefits?

To address these questions, this book is divided into two parts. In part I, we look at the evolution of work and the status of key technologies that are poised to shape its future. Part II suggests how to shape policy, technology, and labor institutions toward shared prosperity.

We start with an essential observation: No compelling historical or contemporary evidence suggests that technological advances are driving us toward a jobless future. On the contrary, we anticipate that in the next two decades, industrialized countries will have more job openings than workers to fill them, and that robotics and automation will play an increasingly crucial role in closing these gaps. Nevertheless, the implications of robotics and automation for workers will not be benign. These technologies, in concert with economic incentives, policy choices, and institutional forces, will alter the set of jobs available and the skills they demand.

This process is both challenging and indispensable. Inventing new ways of accomplishing existing work, new business models, and entirely new industries drives rising productivity and new jobs. Such innovations bring new occupations to life, generate demands for new forms of expertise, and create opportunities for rewarding work. Most of today's jobs hadn't even been invented in 1940. The US needs not less but more technological innovation to meet humanity's most pressing problems, including climate change, disease, poverty, malnutrition, and inadequate education. Mastering these challenges through investment and innovation will create opportunity and improve well-being.

A second key observation is that the momentous impacts of technological change are unfolding gradually.

Spectacular advances in computing and communications, robotics and AI are reshaping industries as diverse as insurance, retail, health care, manufacturing, logistics, and transportation. But we observe substantial time lags, often on the scale of decades, from the birth of an invention to its broad commercialization, assimilation into business processes, widespread adoption, and impacts on the workforce. We find examples of this incremental pace of change in the adoption of novel industrial robots in small and medium-sized firms, and in the still imminent large-scale deployments of autonomous vehicles. Indeed, the most profound labor market effects of new technology that we found were due less to robotics and AI than to the continuing diffusion of decades-old (though much improved) technologies of the internet, mobile and cloud computing, and mobile phones.

This time scale of technological change provides the opportunity to craft policies, develop skills, and foment investments to constructively shape the trajectory of change toward the greatest social and economic benefit.

Part II of this book looks at what will be required to reshape and refocus the institutions and policies of the US to create the shared prosperity that is possible if we are willing to make the necessary changes.

We begin by looking at how workers are trained to make their way in a fast-changing economy. Enabling workers to remain productive in a continuously evolving workplace requires empowering them with excellent skills programs at all stages of life—in primary and secondary schools, in vocational and college programs, and in ongoing adult training programs. The distinctive US system for worker training has shortcomings, but it also has unique virtues. For example, it offers numerous points of entry for workers who may want to reshape their career paths or need to find new work after a layoff. We argue that the US must invest in existing educational and training institutions and innovate to create new training models to make ongoing skills development accessible, engaging, and cost-effective.

But even well-trained and motivated workers need and deserve a sense of basic security. Rising labor productivity has not translated into broad increases in incomes because labor market institutions and policies have fallen into disrepair.

Peer nations from Sweden to Germany to Canada have faced the same economic, technological, and global forces as the US, and have enjoyed equally strong economic growth, but have delivered better results for their workers. What sets the US apart are US-specific institutional changes and policy choices that failed to blunt, and in some cases magnified, the consequences of these pressures on the US labor market.

The US has allowed traditional channels of worker voice to atrophy without fostering new institutions or buttressing existing ones. It has permitted the federal minimum wage to recede to near irrelevance, lowering the floor under the labor market for low-paid workers. It has embraced a policy-driven expansion of free trade with the developing world, Mexico and China in particular, that has raised aggregate national income, and yet it has failed to redress the employment losses and retraining needs of workers displaced by these expansions.

No evidence suggests that this strategy of embracing growth while ignoring the plight of rank-and-file workers has paid off for the United States. US leadership in growth and innovation is long-standing: It led the world throughout the twentieth century, and led even more definitively in the several decades immediately after World War II. Conversely, the labor market maladies documented here are recent. Nothing suggests that these failures inevitably follow from innovation or constitute costs worth paying to gain the other economic benefits that they ostensibly deliver. We can do better.

In the absence of deliberate policy, good jobs are undersupplied by markets and yet have broad social and political benefits, especially in a democracy. Work is a crucial human good. "Not simply a source of income," Task Force Research Advisory Board member Josh Cohen writes in an MIT Work of the Future research brief, "work is a way that we can learn, exercise our powers of perception, imagination, and judgment, collaborate socially, and make constructive social contributions."[1] Even when work is solely a means of acquiring an income, it should offer a sense of purpose and not require submission to demeaning or arbitrary authority, unhealthy or unsafe conditions, or physical or mental degradation.

Recognizing the centrality of good jobs to human welfare and the centrality of innovation to the creation of good jobs leads us to ask how we can leverage investments in innovation to drive job creation, speed growth, and meet rising competitive challenges.

Investments in innovation grow the economic pie, which is crucial to meeting challenges posed by a globalized and fiercely technologically competitive world economy. Throughout our studies, we found technologies that were direct results of US federal investment in research and development over the past century and longer: the internet, advanced semiconductors, AI, robotics, and autonomous vehicles, to name but a few. These new goods and services generate new industries and occupations that demand new skills and offer new earnings opportunities. The US has a stellar record of supporting innovations that inventors, entrepreneurs, and creative capital deploy to support and create new businesses.

Adopting new technology creates winners and losers and will continue to do so. The involvement of all stakeholders—including workers, businesses, investors, educational and nonprofit organizations, and government—can minimize the harms and maximize the benefits to individuals and communities and help ensure that the labor market of the future offers benefits, opportunity, and a measure of economic security to all.

2

LABOR MARKETS AND GROWTH

We envision a labor market that, in concert with rapidly advancing automation and computation, offers dignity, opportunity, and economic security for workers. How can we make that labor market a reality? Research in multiple fields, from economics and engineering to history and political science, tells us how we got here and offers some glimpses of possible futures. This chapter draws lessons from that work and synthesizes them to point toward ways forward.

TWO FACES OF TECHNOLOGICAL CHANGE: TASK AUTOMATION AND NEW WORK CREATION

Technological change enables people to accomplish previously infeasible tasks or to perform conventional tasks with greater efficiency. Such changes have helped elevate humanity from the continual threats of darkness, hunger, illness, physical dangers, and backbreaking labor over multiple centuries.[1]

This technological progress is desirable, indeed essential, for addressing humanity's most pressing problems, including climate change, disease, poverty, malnutrition, and lack of education.

But technological advances do not necessarily benefit everyone, let alone all workers. The majority of adults in industrialized countries are currently able to escape poverty by working in paid employment. But this state of affairs is exceptional and should not be taken for granted.[2] Does technological change, and automation in particular, threaten this favorable arrangement?

The threat could take two forms. First, automation could ultimately reduce the number of jobs in which humans are more productive than machines, spurring mass unemployment.[3] Second, automation could reshape job skill demands such that a minority of workers with highly specialized skills earn outsized rewards while the majority of citizens lose ground.

The first possibility—the end of work—runs contrary to the evidence. Even as technological advances have made life longer, more comfortable, and more interesting, they have generally led to net job creation rather than net job destruction. If automation (or its predecessor, mechanization) tends to render human labor redundant, we would have expected paid employment to decline during the twentieth century—arguably the most technologically progressive period in recorded human history—as automation necessitated successive reallocations of workers out of agriculture and into industry, and then into services. But the opposite occurred: The fraction of US adults working in paid employment rose during almost every decade between 1890 and 2000.[4] Indeed, in the vast body of economic research on automation and employment, no rigorous evidence suggests that automation has caused aggregate employment to fall over a sustained time period.[5] Moreover, even as concern about technological unemployment has risen in recent years, the industrialized world has seen sustained rapid employment growth.

While no economic law dictates that the creation of new work must equal or exceed the elimination of old work, history shows that they tend to evolve together.[6] Indeed, as detailed in the next chapter, in each instance where the Task Force focused its expertise on specific technologies, we found technological change—while visible and auguring vast potential—is moving less rapidly, and displacing fewer jobs, than portrayed in popular accounts. New technologies themselves are often astounding, but it can take decades from the birth of an invention to its commercialization, assimilation into business processes, standardization, widespread adoption, and broader impacts on the workforce. This evolutionary pace of change opens up opportunities to craft policies, develop skills, and foment investments to shape the trajectory of change to create broader social and economic benefits.

These facts pose a paradox. Since automation "saves labor"—displacing workers from specific tasks and occupations (e.g., harvesting corn)—why hasn't it reduced employment in total? The most credible answer is that even as automation saves labor, it spurs three countervailing forces that tend to generate new work. First, automation makes workers more productive in the tasks that are not automated: roofers wield pneumatic nail guns to hang shingles, doctors deploy panels of tests to make diagnoses, architects rapidly render designs, teachers deliver lessons through telepresence, filmmakers use computer graphics to simulate unworldly action sequences, and long-haul truck drivers upload their route to cloud-based dispatching platforms to ensure they never ride with an empty load. In each of these instances, automation of a subset of tasks augments the productivity of workers accomplishing larger objectives by vastly increasing their efficiency.

Second, automation drives productivity increases that raise total income in the economy. Much of this income is then spent on additional goods and services—larger houses, safer vehicles, better meals and entertainment, more frequent and more distant travel, further education, and more comprehensive health care. This additional consumption demands workers and hence raises employment.

Finally, and perhaps most profoundly, even as automation eliminates human labor from certain tasks, technological change leads to new kinds of work. New goods and services, new industries and occupations demand new skills and offer new earnings opportunities. A century ago, there was no computer industry, there were no solar energy jobs or television networks, and air travel was in its infancy. Automobiles, electrification, and home telephones were only just becoming commonplace. In the past century, new industries, products, and services have generated vast numbers of new jobs, often demanding higher skill levels and paying higher wages than those that preceded them. These innovations transformed the economy.

Consider the set of jobs available to workers in 1940 as compared to those active today, as shown in figure 2.1. In 2018, 63 percent of jobs in

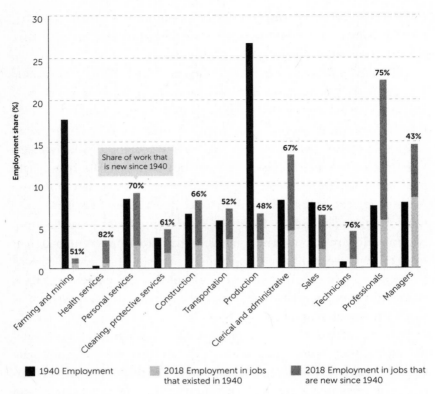

Figure 2.1
More Than 60 Percent of Jobs Done in 2018 Had Not Yet Been "Invented" in 1940. The distribution of employment in 1940 and 2018 across major occupations, distinguishing job categories added between 1940 and 2018 job categories present in 1940. *Source:* David Autor, Anna Salomons, and Bryan Seegmiller, "New Frontiers: The Origins and Content of New Work, 1940–2018," mimeo, MIT Department of Economics, 2021.

new occupational titles had not yet been "invented" as of 1940.[7] Many of these new jobs were directly enabled by technology, including jobs in information technology (IT); solar and wind power; the engineering, design, installation, and repair of new products; and new medical specialties.

But not all new work is in "high-tech" jobs. Some is found in in-person service jobs, such as mental health counselors, chat room hosts, sommeliers, home health aides, and fitness coaches. These roles partly reflect new demands stemming from rising incomes (an indirect effect of rising productivity) and the novel needs of individuals in an industrialized society. Meanwhile, traditional sectors, such as agriculture and production, have created less work, and new occupations have stopped emerging.

Inevitably, jobs recede in some sectors, such as agriculture, as technology advances. In others, such as manufacturing, globalization reduces domestic demand for labor. Sometimes consumer tastes shift. Simultaneously, new work emerges in innovative industries, such as computing, renewable energy, and health care. Rising incomes also create new consumption demands, such as for new fitness clubs.

Many new jobs have their roots in earlier decades of investment. In the second half of the twentieth century, the US built a research and development (R&D) infrastructure that enabled the nation to innovate more rapidly and more effectively than other advanced economies.[8] As a prime example, the computer and internet revolutions of the 1980s and 1990s, as well as the current progress in AI and robotics, stemmed directly from long-term investments by agencies like DARPA (the Defense Advanced Research Projects Agency), the arm of the Pentagon devoted to researching and adopting new technologies. Not only did these investments speed innovation, they provided the training ground for generations of experts and built clusters of employment in high-tech industries that have persisted for decades.

The trajectory of work creation mirrored the direction of innovation throughout the twentieth and twenty-first centuries. The flowering of new occupations and industries shifted from manufacturing and heavy industry in the first decades of the twentieth century to high-tech process-intensive sectors during the post–World War II decades (e.g., photography, metallurgy, material chemistry). In the later decades of the twentieth century, the emergence of new occupations shifted again to instruments, information, and electronics, coinciding with the IT revolution.[9] Innovation spurs job creation, and that innovation is frequently catalyzed, funded, and shaped by public investment.

However, these processes do not benefit everyone. Changes in the structure of work inevitably generate riches for some and hardships for others. Merely to keep pace with shifting product and skill demands, workers, firms, and governments must make costly investments. Recent decades have witnessed sharp declines in such sectors as steel, mining, and textile production that have ushered in concentrated and persistent job loss in communities specializing in these activities.[10] Even if some of these transitions were necessary, such as the ongoing transition from coal to cleaner energy sources, the net benefits do not erase the hardship borne by those who found themselves on the wrong side of the labor demand curve.

This brings us to a central theme of this book: whether rising productivity generates broadly improving living standards or instead enriches a relatively small subset of the population depends on the societal institutions that channel productivity into incomes. These institutions interact with the labor market, which itself accounts for the greatest part of the economy.[11] In this crucial arena, the US has performed poorly along multiple dimensions.

Over the last four decades, wage growth for the majority of US workers has diverged from overall productivity growth. Alongside weak wage growth for rank-and-file workers, this divergence has entailed multiple labor market maladies with enormous social consequences: low-paid, insecure jobs for workers without a college degree, low participation in the labor force, historically high levels of earnings inequality, and festering earnings and employment disparities among races that have not substantially improved in decades.

No single cause accounts for these multiple maladies, but three factors appear most important. First, the advancing digitalization of work has made highly educated workers more productive and less-educated workers easier to replace with machinery. Second, the acceleration of trade and globalization, spurred by surging US imports from China and the rapid outsourcing of US production work, caused a rapid decline of manufacturing employment. Finally, institutions that once enabled rank-and-file workers to bargain for wage growth to match productivity growth have eroded. This erosion is seen in plummeting labor union membership and falling real federal minimum wage levels, which are now approaching historic lows.

These unfavorable outcomes were not an inevitable consequence of technology, globalization or market forces. No other wealthy industrialized country has seen an equally large rise in inequality or equally severe wage stagnation among rank-and-file workers as has the United States.

Boosted by rising education and skill levels, advancing workplace technologies, growing global integration, and numerous accompanying factors, labor productivity in the US has risen steeply. And yet these productivity gains have not translated into broadly based increases in incomes because the supporting societal institutions and labor market policies that perform that function have fallen into disrepair. The US must reinvigorate and modernize those institutions and policies to restore the synergy between rising productivity and improvements in work. The remainder of this chapter delves into the basis for these conclusions.

RISING INEQUALITY AND THE GREAT DIVERGENCE

Starting in the 1960s and continuing through the early 1980s, earnings grew for US workers of both sexes, regardless of education (see figure 2.2). In fact, the US economy delivered stellar, broadly shared growth in the preceding two decades as well, from the end of World War II through the mid-1970s. The growth in earnings was both rapid and evenly

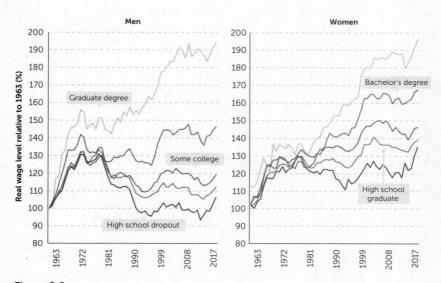

Figure 2.2
Change in Real Wages since 1980. Real wages have risen for college graduates and fallen for workers with a high school degree or less. *Source:* David H. Autor, "Work of the Past, Work of the Future," *AEA Papers and Proceedings* 109 (May 2019): 1–32.

distributed. Between 1948 and 1978, US productivity, measured by total output per hour of work, rose by 108 percent, as shown in figure 2.3, a brisk annual growth rate of 2.4 percent. During the same period, average compensation of production and nonsupervisory workers (a stand-in for the median since median wages are not available for this period) rose in near lockstep, increasing by 95 percent.

This rapid growth in productivity and worker compensation came to a sudden stop in 1973, as shown in figure 2.3. The proximate cause of this sharp halt was an oil embargo imposed by the Organization of Arab Petroleum Exporting Nations (OAPEC), which caused world oil prices to triple in less than a year and threw many industrialized economies into recession.[12] Though the embargo lasted only six months, the trajectory of productivity growth in the US and most advanced countries came to a near standstill for a decade. And when it returned in the early 1980s, it did so at a slower pace than in the three prior decades.[13]

To this day, there is no economic consensus as to why the 1973 oil price shock—which eventually came to be known as the "first oil

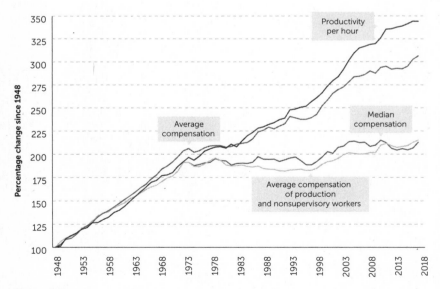

Figure 2.3
Productivity and Compensation Growth in the US, 1948–2016. *Source:* Anna M. Stansbury and Lawrence H. Summers, "Productivity and Pay: Is the Link Broken?," National Bureau of Economic Research Working Paper No. W24165, December 2017, figure 2.

crisis"—appears to have knocked industrialized countries off their steep upward post–World War II productivity growth trajectory.[14] For the purposes of this book, however, the slowdown is less central to the story than is a second crucial economic reality also revealed by figure 2.3: the diverging paths of productivity and compensation growth after the mid-1970s. Whereas productivity and median compensation both approximately doubled between 1948 and 1978, they went their separate ways thereafter. Between 1978 and 2016, aggregate output per hour of work (aka productivity) rose by a further 66 percent, an annual growth rate of 1.3 percent. Yet the compensation of production and nonsupervisory workers rose by a mere 12 percent, and the compensation of the median worker rose by only 11 percent. Simultaneously, *average* worker compensation roughly kept pace with productivity over this period, at least until the early 2000s (a point to which we return below). This growing gulf between rising productivity and stagnating *median* wages is often referred to as "the great divergence."

Within this great divergence lurk multiple dimensions of growing inequality—by education, race, ethnicity, gender, and even geography. Most salient, although median wage growth was tepid across the board, its distribution was nevertheless skewed toward more advantaged workers, specifically white men and women (figure 2.4). Between 1979 and 2018, the median hourly wages of white men rose by 7 percent while those of Black and Hispanic men rose by only 1 percent and 3 percent, respectively. Growth in women's earnings was far stronger, which is certainly a favorable development in light of the large historical (and current) earnings gap between men and women. But again, this gender convergence had a strong racial skew. Median hourly wages among white women rose by 42 percent, whereas they rose by only 25 percent and 26 percent among Black and Hispanic women, respectively.[15]

Could the decoupling between average productivity growth and median wage growth simply mean that the median worker is not getting much more productive while the productivity of high-wage, high-education workers is surging ahead?[16] This idea is challenging to test since economic data measure average productivity of industries and economies, not the productivity of individual workers. Other countries have also experienced rising educational wage differentials and a decoupling between productivity growth and median earnings growth, and this

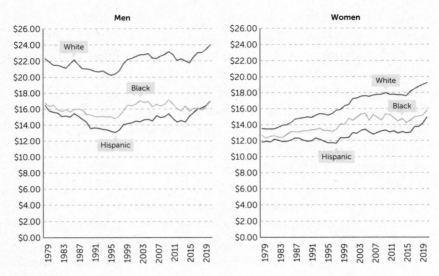

Figure 2.4
Modest Median Wage Increases in the US since 1979. Wage increases have been concentrated among white men and women. *Source:* Economic Policy Institute, State of Working America Data Library, "Median/Average Hourly Wages," 2019, http://www.edpi.org/data/#?subject=wage-avg.

pattern suggests that technological factors that countries have in common—as opposed to institutional factors that they do not—are likely part of the explanation. But the US is an extreme case. Among twenty-four countries for which data are available, the Organization for Economic Cooperation and Development (OECD) reports that the US had the third-largest decoupling between productivity growth (1.8 percent) and median wage growth (0.5 percent) between 1995 and 2013, a gap of 1.3 percent, exceeded by only Poland and Korea.[17] By comparison, the gap between productivity growth and median wage growth was less than half as large (0.7 percent) in Canada, the Netherlands, Australia, and Japan, and only one-sixth as large (0.2 percent) in Germany, Austria, and Norway.[18]

If productivity rose but median incomes did not, where did all of that extra productivity go? The answer has two parts. We provide the first half of the answer here and the second a bit later in the chapter. First and foremost, income went *upward*, toward workers earning above the median of the wage distribution. The real wages of workers with four-year college degrees pulled steeply away from the rest of the pack after 1980 (see figure 2.2), and the wages of workers with graduate degrees (e.g., MBAs, MDs, JDs, PhDs) pulled away faster. In fact, real earnings of males with college and post-college degrees rose by 25 to 50 percent between 1980 and 2017. By contrast, real weekly wage earnings among men without a four-year college degree peaked around 1980 and fell over the next several decades. Despite some wage rebound during the high-pressure labor markets of the late 1990s and the few years prior to the COVID-19 pandemic, the average weekly earnings of males with some college, high school, or less than high school education were 10 to 20 percent lower in 2017 than in 1980.

Earnings growth among women was stronger than among men but just as unequal. For women with college or post-college education, real earnings rose steeply, by forty to sixty percentage points, between 1980 and 2017. For women with less than a four-year degree, however, wages rose by no more than ten percent.

The rapid increase in earnings of college-educated workers, and the stagnant earnings of just about everyone else, explains how median compensation could remain stuck in place even as average compensation rose. Indeed, the rising earnings gap between workers with and without four-year college degrees drives a large fraction of the growth of earnings inequality. This gap has grown in almost every industrialized country, though, as in many domains, the US presents an extreme case.[19] Conventional supply and demand forces in part help to explain why. Throughout much of the twentieth century, successive waves of innovation—electrification, mass production, motorized transportation, telecommunications—intensified the demand for formal education, technical expertise, and cognitive ability upward. Boosted by the World War II and Korean War GI bills, these demands were met by a surge in new college graduates.[20] In the 1980s and 1990s, the virtuous coincidence of rising college demand and expanding college supply broke down: College enrollment among young US adults flatlined and even fell in the case of US men, and the college wage premium surged. That premium has exceeded its previous high-water mark, set in 1915, in every year of the twenty-first century.[21]

This history underscores that to boost individual and aggregate productivity, the US must continually invest to raise education and skill levels, as it has done for more than a century. But this history does not

explain why the earnings of the median US worker decoupled from productivity growth four decades ago, even while the education level of that
median worker was rising rapidly.[22]

As median wages have stagnated and incomes of highly educated
workers have risen, ever larger shares of national income have flowed
to the very top earners. Between 1979 and 2018, the share of all pretax national income flowing to the top 10 percent of adults rose from
35 percent to 47 percent—meaning that 10 percent of individual adults
received almost half of all national income. Simultaneously, the share
of national income accruing to the top 1 percent of adults rose from 11
percent to 19 percent, meaning that 1 percent of adults received a fifth of
all income. Meanwhile, the share of total income flowing to the bottom
50 percent of adults declined from 20 percent to 14 percent.[23]

The rise of top incomes has multiple causes, including technology-
fueled "superstar" effects that enable top workers and firms in numerous
sectors to command an outsized market share (e.g., Google, Facebook,
ExxonMobil, Disney, BlackRock), the ratcheting down of top tax rates
that effectively penalized paying extremely high salaries to top executives, and changing norms about what constitutes reasonable pay levels
for executives, managers, and line workers.[24]

The US is again an outlier in both the level of income concentration
and the degree of its increase. Among industrialized anglophone, Western European, and Northern European nations, none approaches the US
in either the share of income accruing to the top 1 percent or the increase
in this share over the past four decades.[25] While tax and transfer policies
could in theory offset rising pretax income concentration, the US does
less to offset inequality through taxation than do most European countries (though, interestingly, not less than Canada or Sweden).[26] The net
result is that the US has higher after-tax inequality, and has seen a steeper
rise, than other industrialized countries.

EMPLOYMENT POLARIZATION AND DIVERGING
JOB QUALITY

One factor that both reflects and contributes to these rising earnings disparities is the polarization of job growth into traditionally high-wage and

traditionally low-wage occupations at the expense of the middle tier. At the high end of the labor market, a growing cadre of high-education, high-wage occupations offers strong career prospects, rising lifetime earnings, and significant employment security. At the other end, low-education, low-wage occupations provide little economic security and limited career earnings growth. Traditional middle-tier jobs in production, machine operation, clerical and administrative support, and sales occupations are in decline (see figure 2.5).

The causes of labor market polarization are well understood. The movement of labor from agriculture to industry to services over the twentieth century has slowly eroded demand for physical labor and raised the centrality of cognitive labor in practically every walk of life. The past four decades of computerization in particular have extended the reach of this process by displacing workers from performing routine, codifiable

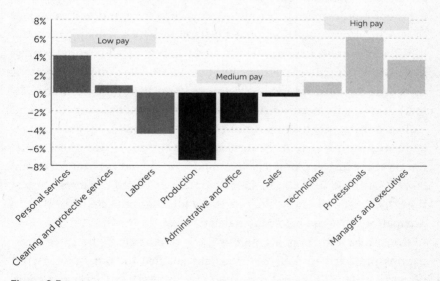

Figure 2.5
Changes in Occupational Employment Shares among Working-Age Adults, 1980–2015. Employment growth has polarized between high- and low-paid occupations. *Sources:* Steven Ruggles, Sarah Flood, Ronald Goeken, et al. Integrated Public Use Microdata Series: Version 8.0 [dataset], University of Minnesota, 2018, http://doi.org/10.18128/ D010.V8.0; U.S. Census of Population data for 1980, 1900, and 2000; American Community Survey (ACS) data for 2014 through 2016; David Dorn, "Essays on Inequality, Spatial Interaction, and the Demand for Skills," PhD diss., Verlag nicht ermittelbar, 2009.

cognitive tasks (e.g., bookkeeping, clerical work, repetitive production tasks) that are now readily scripted with computer software and performed by inexpensive digital machines. This ongoing process of machine substitution for routine human labor tends to increase the productivity of educated workers whose jobs rely on information, calculation, problem solving, and communication—workers in medicine, marketing, design, and research, for example. It simultaneously displaces the middle-skilled workers who in many cases provided these information-gathering, organizational, and calculation tasks. These include sales workers, office workers, administrative support workers, and assembly line production workers.[27]

Ironically, digitalization has had the smallest impact on the tasks of workers in low-paid manual and service jobs, such as food service workers, cleaners, janitors, landscapers, security guards, home health aides, vehicle drivers, and numerous entertainment and recreation workers.[28] Performing these jobs demands physical dexterity, visual recognition, face-to-face communications, and situational adaptability, which remain largely out of reach of current hardware and software but are readily accomplished by adults with modest levels of education. As middle-skilled occupations have declined, manual and service occupations have become an increasingly central job category for those with high school or lower education.

This polarization likely will not come to a halt any time soon. In prepandemic forecasts, the US Bureau of Labor Statistics (BLS) projects that the US will add approximately six million jobs in net between 2019 and 2029.[29] Of those six million, 4.8 million are projected to emerge in just thirty occupations. Two-thirds of those jobs are projected to occur in occupations that pay below the median wage.

Consistent with ongoing employment polarization, the three occupations projected to add the most jobs are tied to in-person services: home health and personal care aides (1.2 million), fast-food and counter workers (0.46 million), and restaurant cooks (0.23 million). The three occupations that are projected to shed the most jobs in net are cashiers, secretaries and administrative assistants, and miscellaneous assemblers and fabricators.[30] The primary duties of all three jobs include performing codifiable information-processing and repetitive assembly tasks that are susceptible to automation.[31]

We stress, however, that while ongoing occupational polarization is eroding employment in middle-skilled production, machine operation, technical, and administrative positions, the US should not stop investing in these types of jobs. Employers will continue to need to hire people for these occupations as workers retire or transition to other sectors. Meanwhile, the rapid expansion of the health care sector will add many middle-skilled jobs in nontraditional occupations, as will the growing category of supply chain firms that provide services to business and government.[32] Jobs such as respiratory therapist, dental hygienist, and clinical laboratory technician offer middle-income salaries to workers with an associate's degree in the relevant field.[33] These fields are strong candidates for targeted training investments.

Employment polarization is not a problem on its own if wages and benefits found in low-paid US occupations enable workers to rise above poverty and attain a reasonable expectation of economic security. But they do not. By almost every measure of job quality—pay, working environment, prior notice of job termination, and access to paid vacation, sick time, and family leave—less-educated and low-paid US workers fare poorly relative to comparably-skilled workers in other wealthy industrialized nations.[34] Figure 2.6 provides one such benchmark, comparing the

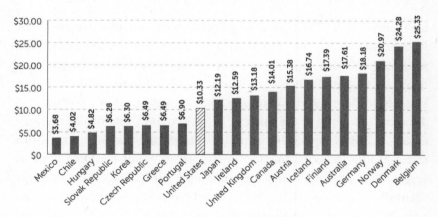

Figure 2.6
PPP-Adjusted Gross Hourly Earnings of Low-Skilled Workers in the US and Other OECD Countries. Low-skilled workers receive lower pay in the US than in other industrialized countries. *Source:* https://stats.oecd.org/Index.aspx?QueryId=82334.

purchasing-power-parity-adjusted gross (pretax) hourly pay of low-skilled workers in twenty-two OECD countries in 2015.[35]

Low-skilled US workers earn only 79 percent as much as low-skilled UK workers, only 74 percent as much as low-skilled Canadian workers, and only 57 percent as much as low-skilled German workers. While no single metric makes for a complete comparison, numerous analyses support the qualitative picture painted by figure 2.6.[36]

A recent *New York Times* article by Nicholas Kristof memorably illustrates the poor standing of low-wage US workers relative to their counterparts in other industrialized countries.[37] Kristof points out that the starting pay for a grill worker at a McDonald's restaurant in Denmark is about $22 an hour. This figure, which includes pay supplements, would shock any fast-food worker in Indiana, California, or anywhere else in the US, including in expensive cities where the "Fight for 15" movement for a higher minimum wage gained momentum. Yet these pay differentials actually understate the true gap in compensation. The McDonald's worker in Denmark receives six weeks of paid vacation a year, life insurance, and a pension. Such benefits are unheard of for starting grill cooks at McDonald's restaurants in the United States.[38]

REBUILDING THE ESCALATOR TO JOB OPPORTUNITIES

Inequality in the US also has a geographic dimension. Over the past three decades, the US has seen steeply rising income levels and bustling prosperity in such cities as New York, San Francisco, and Los Angeles. Job opportunities and higher wages attract highly educated workers to such knowledge centers. Indeed, in contrast to predictions about the "death of distance" as a result of the internet and telecommunications technology, urban areas have become more, not less, attractive, leading to increasing divergence in the economic fortunes of urban versus rural and younger versus older areas. Some mid-sized cities such as Kansas City, Columbus, Charlotte, and Nashville have also benefited from the knowledge economy while leveraging their relative affordability.

Elsewhere, in many once-thriving metropolitan areas in states from Mississippi to Michigan, the situation is more distressing. These regions face economic stagnation, declining employment of adults in their prime working years, and high rates of receipt of federal disability benefits.

Non-college-educated workers used to be able to earn more by moving to cities, but no longer. The economic escalator that US cities once offered to workers of all backgrounds has slowed. Even in the wealthiest US cities, the workforce is increasingly bifurcated. On the one hand, high-wage professionals enjoy the amenities that thriving urban areas can offer. On the other hand, an underclass of less-educated service workers gets by with diminishing purchasing power while attending to the care, comfort, and convenience of the more affluent.

These trends have been particularly harmful to the job prospects of minority workers, who are overrepresented in US cities.[39] Among non-college-educated whites, employment in mid-paying occupations fell by six to eight percentage points in urban relative to nonurban areas, as shown in figure 2.7. Blacks and Hispanics experienced declines twice as large: twelve to sixteen percentage points. In all cases, these falls in mid-pay employment were matched by a rise in low-pay employment.

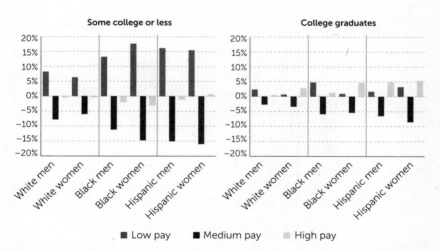

Figure 2.7
Changes in Occupational Employment Shares in Urban versus Nonurban Labor Markets by Education, Gender, and Race or Ethnicity, 1980–2015. Urban occupational polarization has been much greater among minority workers. *Source:* David Autor, "The Faltering Escalator of Urban Opportunity," MIT Work of the Future Research Brief, July 2020.

The data show no upward occupational mobility among non-college-educated urban workers. Moreover, although occupational polarization is less pronounced among college-educated urban workers, it is again more than twice as large among Black and Hispanic than among white college graduates.[40]

As jobs in urban areas have polarized, the urban wage premium for non-college-educated workers has fallen, and the decline has been greatest among Black and Hispanic workers (see figure 2.8). The urban differential dropped by five to seven percentage points among non-college-educated Hispanics and by twelve to sixteen percentage points among non-college-educated Blacks.[41] Conversely, there was almost no decline among non-college-educated whites. And even among college-educated workers, where the urban wage premium generally rose, minorities fared less well. Gains were larger for whites of both sexes than for Blacks and Hispanics of either sex. And, consistent with the adverse occupational shifts plotted above, urban Black college-educated men saw their wages fall relative

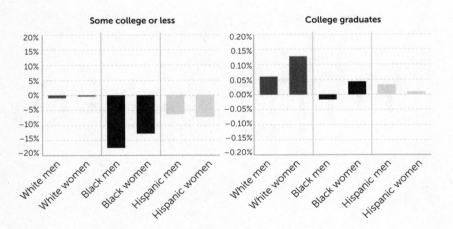

Figure 2.8
Differential Urban Wage Polarization among Minorities in Urban Labor Markets, 1980–2015. Figure shows percentage changes in real wage levels (not adjusting for local cost of living) in urban versus nonurban labor markets by education, gender, and race or ethnicity, 1980–2015. The urban wage premium has fallen much more among minority workers. *Source:* David Autor, "The Faltering Escalator of Urban Opportunity," MIT Work of the Future Research Brief, July 2020.

to their nonurban counterparts—a distressing result that deserves deeper study than we can offer here.

LABOR'S FALLING SHARE OF NATIONAL INCOME

We noted above that there is a two-part answer to the question of "Where did all of the productivity go?" Rising inequality is the first part of the answer. The second is a falling share of labor compensation in national income. Starting around the year 2000, the growth of *both* median compensation and *average* compensation fell behind the growth of aggregate productivity (also seen in figure 2.3). By implication, the share of economic output paid to workers as a group (what is commonly known as "labor's share") declined while, correspondingly, the share of economic output paid to capital and profits rose. In fact, labor's share has dropped by about seven percentage points in the US since the year 2000 (a steep fall), and has fallen to a lesser but nonnegligible degree in many other industrialized countries.[42]

What makes this development especially startling is that throughout much of the twentieth century, the division of national income between workers, in the form of wages and compensation, and capital, in the form of rents and profits, appeared so stable that it came to be seen as something like an economic law: two-thirds of income goes to labor, one-third to capital.[43] But that law has been repeatedly violated over the last two decades, and arguably repealed, to the detriment of workers, who now receive a shrinking share of a not very rapidly growing pie. While there is not yet an economic consensus as to why labor's share is falling, understanding the possible causes helps to illuminate the many forces that may shape the distribution of income.

One prominent explanation is regulatory failure, specifically, that antitrust authorities have been too lax in preventing large firms from dominating their sectors and quashing competition in such areas as internet search, social networking, computers, electronics and mobile devices, broadband and wireless services, air transportation, health insurance, and appliances.[44] The problem with dominant firms is that they use their market power to command prices that are far above competitive levels, and these high prices yield abnormally large profits. In an earlier era, when labor unions had more bargaining power, these profits might have been distributed among rank-and-file workers, managers, and corporate owners (including shareholders). In the current era, however, when labor unions are historically weak (as we discuss later), these profits flow primarily to corporate owners through higher stock prices, dividend payouts, and after-tax profits. The net result is that rising market dominance fuels a decline in labor's share of national income.[45]

One limitation of this line of argument is that the decline in labor share appears to have occurred in a large number of countries simultaneously. Because it seems unlikely that most countries relaxed their antitrust enforcement at the same time, this observation suggests that there might be a common cause that has eroded the labor share across many countries simultaneously.[46] One candidate for this common cause is technologies such as robotics and AI, which are rapidly gaining human like capabilities. If these technologies are displacing workers from existing tasks without generating an offsetting group of new labor-using tasks, this will cause labor's share of national income to fall. A key piece of evidence supporting this argument is that the labor share has fallen faster in the sectors that use robotics most intensively, including mining, petroleum and coal production, automotive manufacturing, and electronics.[47] At the level of individual firms, research also finds that when individual plants adopt robotics, they reduce the share of revenues paid to labor.[48] This evidence is compelling, but it is not yet clear how broadly it applies—beyond the important but finite realm of industrial robotics, of course. Indeed, one fact uncovered by a number of recent studies is that the labor share has *not* fallen at the typical (median) firm in most industries, as one might expect if automation were displacing workers broadly.[49]

How can it be that labor share is *not* falling at most firms and yet it is falling in aggregate? This can occur if firms that are *already* capital-intensive rather than labor-intensive—meaning they have low labor shares—gain increasing weight in the economy. This hypothesis, sometimes referred to as the "superstar firm" phenomenon, underscores how technological change can reshape broad economic outcomes in subtle but consequential ways. Here's how it works.

It is widely documented that large firms are more capital- and automation-intensive than average. Relative to competitors, they are typically more productive, more profitable, and pay a larger share of income to capital and profits and a smaller share to labor. Now consider that increasingly sophisticated online and international marketplaces may give a growing edge to firms with a small productivity or cost advantage. This can occur because price competition in online marketplaces is so intense that firms with a small cost advantage can capture large market shares. Alternatively, it may arise because big firms are able to produce sophisticated products at scale—smartphone operating systems, search services, social networks, health insurance plans—something that smaller firms cannot profitably emulate. In either case, the net effect is that economic activity is increasingly concentrated among superstar firms that pay a smaller share of income to labor and larger share to capital and profits. Recent evidence suggests that this has in fact occurred: large firms are capturing a growing share of sales across many industries, pushing out their smaller competitors that are more labor-intensive and less capital-intensive, and pushing down labor's share of national income in the process.

The decoupling between productivity and compensation growth documented above becomes even more keenly felt when productivity growth decelerates, as has occurred in the US and many industrialized countries since approximately 2005: not only is the economic pie growing more slowly than in past decades, labor's share of that pie is also shrinking. The net result is that, understandably, workers are left wondering what happened to their just desserts.

IS THE US GETTING A POSITIVE RETURN ON ITS INEQUALITY?

Could the US have done better for rank-and-file workers over the last four decades? To some readers, the answer is self-evidently yes. But those who view the US economy through a laissez-faire lens may disagree: From this vantage point, the extreme inequality of market outcomes in the US was a necessary condition—and perhaps a worthy price to pay—for the dynamism, economic mobility, and outsized economic growth that the US economy delivers. By this reasoning, the US could not have done better without sacrificing other desirable outcomes.

Is this claim correct? Studies of different countries that examine whether inequality helps or hurts economic growth are inconclusive.[50] Still, the data support a more straightforward conclusion for the US: the nation is getting a low "return" on its inequality.

The unfavorable returns on inequality in the US manifest in multiple ways. Consider first the share of the working-age population that is employed. A common economic presumption is that countries that do not tolerate high levels of inequality will instead have low employment rates because workers with low productivity will be "priced out" of the labor market by high wage floors—that is, made unemployable. By this reasoning, the US should enjoy something closer to full employment than peer nations because it has almost no wage floors. The data do not bear out this prediction, however. The employment rates of both men and women in the United States are decidedly middle of the pack and have fallen sharply over the last two decades relative to those in peer countries (e.g., Canada, Germany, the UK, Sweden).

Consider a second metric of economic performance: upward mobility between generations. Among industrialized countries, the US stands out for its extremes of rich and poor. Indeed, to locate another large country with greater inequality, one must expand the set to include less-developed nations such as China or Brazil. If high US inequality and accompanying economic dynamism provided US children with better odds of ascending the economic ladder over their lifetimes, the US ought to score high on inequality and low on immobility. Figure 2.9 shows that the reverse is true. The US has one of the lowest rates of intergenerational mobility among wealthy democratic countries, considerably below that of France, Germany, Sweden, Australia, or Canada. As highlighted by Chetty and co-workers,[51] the likelihood that a child born to parents in the bottom fifth of the income distribution will reach the top fifth in adulthood is actually about twice as high in Canada (13.5 percent) as in the United States.[52] Upward mobility is not a dividend that the US receives on its outsized inequality.

While robust intergenerational mobility does not necessarily imply a strong labor market or vice versa, these two outcomes are surprisingly closely connected. Research has shown that the decline in absolute mobility in the US across generations is almost perfectly predicted by the

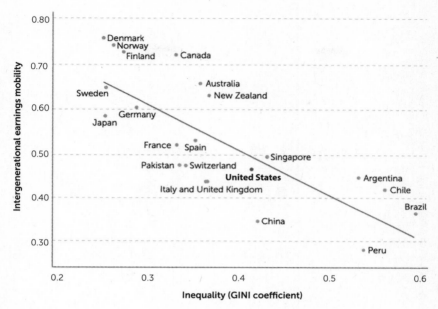

Figure 2.9

Across Countries, Greater Earnings Inequality Is Associated with Lower Intergenerational Economic Mobility. *Source:* Miles Corak, "Inequality from Generation to Generation: The United States in Comparison," in *The Economics of Inequality, Poverty, and Discrimination in the 21st Century,* ed. Robert Rycroft (Santa Barbara, CA: ABC-CLIO, 2013).

growth in the real median income levels of young adults across generations.[53] When median incomes were rising strongly across generations, as was the case in the decades immediately after World War II, absolute income mobility rates were high. When cross-generational growth in median wages flatlined, absolute economic mobility fell in tandem.

A third place to look for an outsized "return" on US inequality is faster economic growth. In general, poorer countries grow faster than rich countries—with important exceptions—as they ride the coattails of key innovations emanating from the rich world (e.g., electrification, telecommunications, medicine). Since rich countries have no coattails to ride, they tend to grow more slowly. This catch-up phenomenon explains the L-shaped relationship seen in figure 2.10 between the initial GDP level of countries in 1960 and their subsequent GDP growth between 1960 and

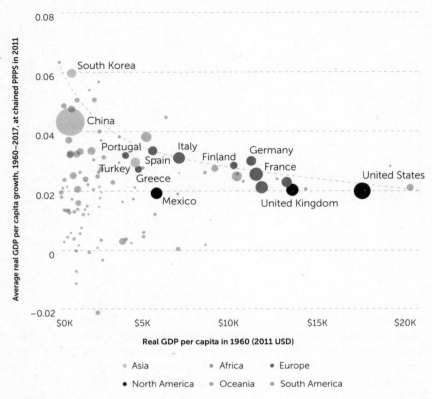

Figure 2.10
Average GDP Growth Rate in 1960–2011 versus GDP per capita in 1960. Countries that were wealthier in 1960 grew less rapidly over the next four decades. *Sources:* Robert C. Feenstra, Robert Inlaar, and Marcel B. Timmer, "The Next Generation of the Penn World Table," *American Economic Review* 105, no. 10 (2015): 3150–3182; Penn World Tables 9.1, Population (Gapminder, HYDE [2016] and UN [2019]).

2011. The US was by far the richest country in 1960, and it experienced the slowest overall growth rate between 1960 and 2011, compared to all other major European, Asian, and North American countries. Countries that were far poorer in 1960 grew on average substantially faster. If, contrary to this logic, one had anticipated that by dint of its economic dynamism, the US would grow faster than other industrialized countries, nothing in this figure suggests that it delivered on that promise.

There have been periods in recent history where the US has grown faster than its European peers, for example during the "dot-com" boom of the mid-1990s.[54] But judged by the most recent half-century of economic data, the US does not stand out from its peers. Moreover, productivity has slowed markedly across industrialized countries since the mid-2000s for reasons that remain poorly understood.[55] Unfortunately, the US is also not an outlier on this dimension: Its productivity growth has decelerated in parallel with that of other advanced countries.

Although the US labor market has delivered little to rank-and-file workers in recent decades, one should not lose sight of the strengths of the US innovation ecosystem. The US remains by almost any measure the most innovative economy in the world. It is plausible that the US business culture of entrepreneurship and risk-taking correlates with the extremes of inequality seen at the top of the US income distribution.[56] This culture of innovation has benefited the United States historically and continues to benefit the country today. At the same time, the significant economic disadvantages and insecurity faced by a substantial share of the US working population almost surely hinder opportunity and mobility. They thwart the investments that individuals, families, and communities would otherwise make in the education, health, and safety of themselves and their children.

Would the US have to forfeit its culture of innovation to ensure that the gains of economic growth redound to the pay, working conditions, and economic security of rank-and-file workers? No evidence suggests that the US faces such a trade-off.[57] US leadership in innovation is long-standing: the country led the world throughout the twentieth century, and led even more definitively in the several decades immediately after World War II. Conversely, the labor market maladies documented above—poor job quality, anemic wage growth, and the decoupling of productivity and wage growth—are recent. Nothing suggests that these failures inevitably follow from innovation or constitute costs worth paying to gain the other economic benefits that they ostensibly deliver.

WHY DID US WORKERS FARE SO POORLY DESPITE RISING PRODUCTIVITY?

Why has the US failed, over the past four decades, to translate rising productivity into improved job opportunities and higher earnings for the majority of workers? Three forces contributed: technological change, globalization pressures, and institutional changes.

Technological change has been a central driver of the rising wage premium paid to formal skills and expertise. By enabling a digitalization of work, computers and the internet have made highly educated workers more productive and less-educated workers easier to replace with machinery. This should not come as a surprise, as IT has significant genealogy in managerial techniques designed to wrest control away from workers and toward abstract processes. Digitalization has also likely contributed to— though does not solely explain—the rising concentration of top incomes. By allowing innovative ideas to scale up rapidly (e.g., in software, in finance, in entertainment, in unique business models such as Amazon or Facebook), digitalization has enabled entrepreneurs to amass vast fortunes. Just as important, the multiplier effect of a networked world has created outsized rewards for top talent in many sectors, such as medicine, law, design, finance, and entertainment.[58]

International trade has also played an important role. China's admission to the World Trade Organization in 2001 spurred the loss of at least one million US manufacturing jobs during the first decade of the 2000s, and that number is larger still if one includes the impacts outside manufacturing. In the US, these job losses were highly concentrated in local labor markets, many in the South Atlantic and South Central regions of the US. In these trade-exposed labor markets, the China trade shock generated sustained adverse impacts on employment rates, household incomes, and other measures of population distress. It further contributed to the political polarization that is currently playing out at all levels of US politics.[59] Thus, although China's emergence as a global economic power was driven by domestic developments within China, the speed and magnitude of the China trade shock on US labor markets were, unlike the impacts of digitalization, a direct outgrowth of US policy.[60]

Similar pressures from digitalization and globalization affected most industrialized countries. What sets the US apart? US-specific institutional changes and policy choices failed to blunt—and in some cases magnified— the consequences of these pressures on the US labor market:[61]

First, the capacity of rank-and-file workers to bargain for wage growth to match productivity growth was hobbled by a steep, sustained fall in union representation. Between 1979 and 2017, the fraction of US workers covered by collective bargaining agreements fell from 26 percent to 12 percent. And this fall was even steeper in the private sector: from 21 percent of workers in 1979 to 6 percent in 2019.[62] Although union representation has generally trended downward in all industrialized countries, no other peer country aside from the UK—which also witnessed an outsized rise in inequality—has seen such a large proportional drop in union coverage or reached such a low level. This fall in turn has numerous causes: a shift of employment away from the traditionally union-heavy manufacturing sector; rising employer resistance to union-organizing efforts, enabled in part by weakening enforcement of collective bargaining protections by the US National Labor Relations Board; growing international competition throughout the post–World War II era that placed US workers in closer competition with their foreign counterparts; and a nearly nine-decades-old collective bargaining framework, the 1935 Wagner Act, that made it difficult for US unions and other worker representatives to adapt to a rapidly changing, increasingly service-based economy.

The second source that magnified pressures on the labor market in the US is a minimum wage that has not kept pace with inflation. In the face of strong ideological and business resistance, successive US Congresses have allowed the real value of the federal minimum wage to atrophy—with only brief respites during the Clinton and Obama administrations. As of 2020, the real value of the federal minimum wage was essentially at the same level as in 1950, seven decades earlier, and was approximately 35 percent below its real value in 1979. The best available evidence indicates that well-calibrated minimum wages exert modest to undetectable adverse effects on employment, reduce household poverty, and are particularly effective at bolstering the earnings of minority workers, who are overrepresented at the lower tail of the US wage distribution.[63] The erosion of the US federal minimum wage, itself a deliberate policy decision, has magnified US earnings inequality, retarded the earnings growth of low-paid US workers, and likely further weakened the hand of labor unions in negotiating on behalf of their members.

Third, US labor policies are leftovers from an earlier era. Congress failed to modernize US labor and social policies to extend conventional protections, like those afforded to direct-hire employees, to the growing ranks of contract, temporary, and gig workers. It also failed to increase the availability and flexibility of unemployment insurance benefits for those not in full-time employment. Finally, it did not ensure that a basic level of portable health insurance and medical, family, and parental leave was available to all workers. This policy vacuum has fostered what the labor relations scholar David Weil has termed a "fissuring" of the workforce.[64] In the words of Task Force member Christine Walley, "employees find themselves increasingly outsourced, sub-contracted, working part-time or on demand, and with less leverage and fewer worker protections."[65]

A fourth source of pressure on the US labor market has been an expansion of free trade without guardrails. Under both Republican and Democratic administrations, the US has embraced a policy-driven expansion of free trade with the developing world—Mexico and China in particular—without enacting complementary trade adjustment policies to buffer the earnings and employment losses and provide for the full range of retraining needs of workers and communities facing sudden policy-induced changes in competitive conditions. While we venerate the core economic insight that trade expansion lowers consumer prices, opens new markets for producers, and fosters the creation of new products and services, the value of these collective benefits provides an even stronger case for assisting workers and communities that are badly hurt by trade policy. The failure of the US to provide such assistance has yielded greater economic, social, and political damage than any plausible cost of the policies that the US might have enacted.

In light of the great divergence in the labor market and the role of technology, particularly IT, in exacerbating that divergence, concerns about new technologies such as AI, robotics, autonomous vehicles, and advanced manufacturing take on a new salience. Will these technologies ease or intensify problems in today's labor market? Or, as people have asked the Task Force, "Will a robot take my job?"

3

TECHNOLOGIES AND INNOVATION

Will a rapid wave of human-like AI put us all out of work? Will algorithms and dexterous robotics hobble growth in low-wage work in the service economy (or replace workers displaced by COVID-19)? Will robots soon be packing our boxes and caring for the elderly?

We don't know precisely. Technological development constantly surprises us. We do know the future will contain a mix of technologies and a mix of approaches across firms large and small. As the previous chapter showed, we also know that new technologies will evolve within a nation of empowered high-skilled work, increasing inequality, eroded worker voice, and racial disparities. Just as policies shape trade and labor institutions, they also shape technology. They shape the rate and manner in which firms develop and adopt technologies, as do organizational cultures, economic incentives, and management practices.

Anxieties about "robots" also express broader cultural unease.[1] Even before COVID-19, middle-class and working-class Americans, especially those without postsecondary education or specialized skills, had ample cause for worry, given the march toward increasingly precarious forms of labor. The US has a poor record of tending to the needs of workers and communities left behind by technological change. The reasons for these economic transformations remain opaque to the public, making it tempting to focus on iconic "robot" machines that conform to familiar

narratives of technology out of control as embodiments of broader, sub-
tler changes.

One reason the 2018 wave of concern about technology and work
seemed so salient is that AI threatens to displace work requiring judgment and expertise in the way earlier waves of automation and computerization displaced repetitive physical and cognitive work. Several reports
point to highly specialized office workers—including, for example, insurance adjusters, paralegals, and accountants—as subject to automation
and worker displacement. The Task Force brief by Thomas W. Malone,
Task Force member Daniela Rus, and Robert Laubacher reviews these
challenges of AI and considers what may lie ahead.[2]

We also know that the future is not etched into machines and algorithms by laws of mathematics or physics. Myriad moments in the processes of technological change enable, indeed require, human choices to
shape the outcome. Engineers encode social relationships and preferred
futures into the machines they build. And economic incentives, R&D
programs, and organizational choices are at least as powerful as engineering visions in shaping the evolution of new technologies. Autonomous
vehicle technology, for example, drew on decades of federal support from
DARPA and other agencies, legacies that still inflect the technology. Similarly, we've witnessed the seismic shift to the use of telepresence tools by
companies, schools, and governments during the COVID-19 pandemic
as the public health crisis inflects development and adoption. Decisions
made by R&D program managers, directors in boardrooms, planners in
offices, and managers on shop floors also determine how jobs evolve as
new tools emerge and become widely available.

Management practices also shape the rate and nature of adoption
of new technologies. As Ari Bronsoler, Joseph Doyle, and Task Force
member John Van Reenen outline in their research brief on health care
IT, engaging workers early in the process of integrating and adapting
workplace technologies promotes acceptance of the new systems and
improves their functioning.[3] Conversely, the top-down imposition
of new technologies and ways of working is often counterproductive.
Stakeholders can resist change, especially when there are large differences between the IT decision-makers (e.g., senior managers) and those
who are using the tools (e.g., physicians, nurses). The researchers find

that greater worker involvement in harnessing the new capabilities of health IT throughout the health care system could improve the acceptance of these technologies while speeding productivity gains and mitigating negative workforce effects.

This chapter synthesizes research from the Task Force that explores the status of key technologies and assesses their implications for jobs: AI in business processes in insurance and health care, autonomous vehicles, robotics in manufacturing and distribution, and additive manufacturing. Some of these technologies, such as autonomous vehicles, are far from widespread use so it remains speculative to forecast how jobs will be reshaped, other than to forecast general timelines and gradual transformation in a decade or more. In other cases we have a clearer sense because forms of the technology are already being adopted, such as the robots that now increasingly carry goods through warehouses. Others are harder to visualize because they involve the use of software to read documents and claims, scan medical prescriptions, or follow transactions to flag potential fraud. All draw on long periods of federally supported basic research to cultivate their genesis and infancy, and to train their practitioners for industry.

Three key themes emerge from this research. First, AI and robotic applications take time to develop and deploy, especially in safety- and production-critical applications. Though they are coming, they are not as close as some would fear, offering some glimpses of potential futures and time for preparation. Flexibility in dynamic environments remains a key human attribute still largely out of reach for machines. This gradualism offers an opportunity to consider how to adopt new technologies for the greatest social and economic benefit. That said, if these technologies are deployed in an economy run according to our existing inadequate labor institutions, they could easily make current trends worse: technological change where benefits narrowly accrue to employers and the most highly educated workers, leaving rank-and-file workers with little gain.

Second, technologies offer mixes of job replacement and augmentation, reflecting a variety of factors. In one case discussed below, legal auditors found that AI helped them in their work, freeing their time for higher-value-added tasks, simultaneously requiring a firm to hire more auditors and improving efficiency. In other cases, warehouse workers are augmented by mobile robots, focusing the human jobs on dexterous tasks that robots cannot do today.

Finally, organizations have a great deal of influence over how technologies are deployed and adopted, and hence over how policies that affect organizations will shape technology. Integration and adaptation are costly and time-consuming tasks in the deployment of any technology to support a particular business. Innovations in these phases of the technology curve can be technical, such as easier programming and standardized interfaces, or organizational, such as engaging front-line workers to fine-tune robotic tasks. In both cases, integration and adaptation crucially link technological change to higher productivity and a labor market that can provide opportunity, mobility, and a measure of economic security to the majority of workers.

FUTURES ARE HERE TODAY: TECHNOLOGY'S LONG CYCLE

To address the first theme, the time to develop and deploy AI and robotic applications, it is worth considering the nature of technological change over time. When people think of new technologies, they often think of Moore's Law, the apparently miraculous doubling of power of microprocessors, or phenomena like the astonishing proliferation of smartphones and apps in the past decades, and their profound social implications. It has become common practice among techno-pundits to describe these changes as "accelerating," though with little agreement on the measures.

But when researchers look at historical patterns, they often find long gestation periods before these apparent accelerations, often three or four decades. Interchangeable parts production enabled the massive gun manufacturing of the Civil War, for example, but it was the culmination of four decades of development and experimentation. After that war, four more decades would pass before those manufacturing techniques matured to enable the innovations of assembly-line production. The Wright Brothers first flew in 1903, but despite the military application of World War I, it was the 1930s before aviation saw the beginnings of profitable commercial transport, and another few decades before aviation matured to the point that ordinary people could fly regularly and safely. Moreover, the expected natural evolution toward supersonic passenger flight hardly materialized, while the technology evolved toward automation, efficiency, and safety at subsonic speeds—dramatic progress, but along other axes than the raw measure of speed.

More recently, the basic technologies of the internet began in the 1960s and 1970s, then exploded into the commercial world in the mid-1990s. Even so, it is only in the past decade that most businesses have truly embraced networked computing as a transformation of their businesses and processes. Task Force member Erik Brynjolfsson calls this phenomenon a "J-curve," suggesting that the path of technological acceptance is slow and incremental at first, then accelerates to break through into broad acceptance, at least for general-purpose technologies like computing.[4] A timeline of this sort reflects a combination of perfecting and maturing new technologies, the costs of integration and managerial adoption, and then fundamental transformations.

While approximate, four decades is a useful time period to keep in mind as we evaluate the relationship of technological change to the future of work. As the science fiction writer William Gibson famously said, "The future is already here, it's just not evenly distributed." Gibson's idea profoundly links the slow evolution of mass adoption to what we see in the world today. Rather than simply making predictions, with their inevitable bias and poor results, we can look for places in today's world that are leading technological change and extrapolate to broader adoption. Today's automated warehouses likely offer a good glimpse of the future, though they will take time for widespread adoption (and likely will not be representative of all warehouses). The same can be said for today's most automated manufacturing lines, and for the advanced production of high-value parts. Autonomous cars are already fifteen years into their development cycle but just beginning to achieve initial deployment. We can look at those initial deployments for clues about their likely adoption at scale. Therefore, rather than do research on the future, the Task Force took a rigorous, empirical look at technology and work today to make some educated extrapolations.

AI TODAY, AND THE GENERAL INTELLIGENCE OF WORK

Most of the AI systems deployed today, while novel and impressive, still fall into the category of what Task Force member, AI pioneer, and director of MIT's Computer Science and Artificial Intelligence Laboratory (CSAIL)

Daniela Rus calls "specialized AI." That is, they are systems that can solve a limited number of specific problems. They look at vast amounts of data, extract patterns, and make predictions to guide future actions. "Narrow AI solutions exist for a wide range of specific problems," write Rus, MIT Sloan School professor Thomas Malone, and Robert Laubacher of the MIT Center for Collective Intelligence, "and can do a lot to improve efficiency and productivity within the work world."[5] Such systems include IBM's Watson system, which beat human players on the American TV game show *Jeopardy!,* and its descendants in health care, or Google's AlphaGo program, which also bests human players in the game of Go. The systems we explore below in insurance and health care all belong to this class of narrow AI, though they vary in different classes of machine learning, computer vision, natural language processing, or others. Other systems in use today also include more traditional "classic AI" systems, which represent and reason about the world with formalized logic. AI is no single thing but rather a variety of different AIs, in the plural, each with different characteristics, that do not necessarily replicate human intelligence.

Specialized AI systems, through their reliance on largely human-generated data, excel at producing behaviors that mimic human behavior on well-known tasks. They also incorporate human biases. They still have problems with robustness, the ability to perform consistently under changing circumstances (including intentionally introduced noise in the data), and trust, the human belief that an assigned task will be performed correctly every single time. "Because of their lack of robustness," write Malone, Rus, and Laubacher, "many deep neural nets work 'most of the time' which is not acceptable in critical applications." The trust problem is exacerbated by the problem of explainability because today's specialized AI systems are not able to reveal to humans how they reach decisions.

The ability to adapt to entirely novel situations is still an enormous challenge for AI and robotics and a key reason why companies continue to rely on human workers for a variety of tasks. Humans still excel at social interaction, unpredictable physical skills, common sense, and, of course, general intelligence.

From a work perspective, specialized AI systems tend to be task-oriented; that is, they execute limited sets of tasks, more than the full set of activities constituting an occupation. Still, all occupations have some exposure. For example, reading radiographs is a key part of radiologists' jobs, but just one of the dozens of tasks they perform. AI in this case can allow doctors to spend more time on other tasks, such as conducting physical examinations or developing customized treatment plans. In aviation, humans have long relied on automatic pilots to augment their manual control of the plane; these systems have become so sophisticated at automating major phases of flight, however, that pilots can lose their manual touch for the controls, leading in extreme cases to fatal accidents. AI systems have not yet been certified to fly commercial aircraft.

Artificial general intelligence (AGI), the idea of a truly artificial human-like brain, remains a topic of deep research interest but a goal that experts agree is far in the future. A current point of debate around AGI highlights its relevance for work. MIT professor emeritus, robotics pioneer, and Task Force Research Advisory Board member Professor Rodney Brooks argues that the traditional "Turing test" for AI should be updated.[6] The old standard was a computer behind a wall with which a human could hold a textual conversation and find it indistinguishable from another person. This goal was achieved long ago with simple chatbots, which few argue represent AGI.

In a world of robotics, as the digital world increasingly mixes with the physical world, Brooks argues for a new standard for AGI: the ability to do complex work tasks that require other types of interaction with the world. One example might be the work of a home health aide. These tasks include providing physical assistance to a fragile human, observing their behavior, and communicating with family and doctors. Brooks's idea, whether embodied in this particular job, a warehouse worker's job, or other kinds of work, captures the sense that today's intelligence challenges are problems of physical dexterity, social interaction, and judgment as much as they are of symbolic data processing. These dimensions remain out of reach for current AI, which has significant implications for work. Pushing Brooks's idea further, we might say that the future of AI is the future of work.

SOFTWARE: THE ROBOTS YOU DON'T SEE

To explore the current state and future potential of AI in service occupations, MIT researchers did deep dives into the realms of insurance and health care. They found firms experimenting with new software and AI technologies to redesign workflows, revise task allocation, and improve job design, for both higher- and lower-educated workers, with the aim of boosting productivity. The pace of adoption appears uneven across industries and firm sizes. In both the insurance industry and the health care industry, automation is occurring at the task level more so than at the job level, and we are still in the early days of implementation.

Task Force executive director Dr. Elisabeth Reynolds led a team of researchers to look closely at a major insurance company's effort to adopt automated systems.[7] The insurance industry has a long history of leading in information technologies. This company had already experimented with robotic process automation (RPA), which is software that automates rules-based actions performed on a computer, often as an overlay to legacy software systems. The company concluded that RPA hadn't delivered the expected results: Most workers accomplish heterogeneous tasks, and the software was insufficiently flexible to automate all of them. Even people ostensibly doing the same job had different methods or routines for accomplishing them.

So the company reassessed its approach, looking for ways to automate certain functions. Part of the solution included installing chatbots to handle the simplest questions sent to their internal help desk and customer service centers, then training the workers to engage with customers at more meaningful levels.

Overall, automation raised the productivity of the current workforce while reducing the number of workers needed to accomplish the job (though the dynamic may evolve if automation allows the firm to reduce prices or offer better products). Another challenge the company identified was ensuring that such task automation didn't lock employees into old routines and legacy technologies, which could hobble future efforts at innovation.

The dominant force for this firm was digitalization, advanced applications of IT, and cloud computing, not necessarily AI-type algorithms. "Our business is technology," one company leader said. "There isn't a separation now." The firm adopted the new management techniques of agile methods and agile software developed over twenty years by the software industry. Agile methods include small, highly cooperative teams that rapidly execute multiple design iterations (as opposed to larger teams that follow more linear workflows). As a consequence, the firm moved from heavy reliance on two software vendors (IBM and Microsoft) to dozens of smaller, cloud-based platforms. These changes in software development and use have had the deepest impacts on how the firm does business.

By contrast, AI applications have not yet lived up to their promise. Deployment of machine learning–based chatbots for customer service and the use of RPA to increase efficiencies in back-office work represent some of the earliest applications of automation technologies. While the latter is not fundamentally new (the initial development was started after the 1990s), its scope and reach into different sectors and companies that have sizable traditional back-office operations have made it a building block of firms' AI strategies. "Consulting firms did a huge disservice to firms like ours by telling them they could save billions with these new AI functions," one company leader said. "We've used some of this, but it hasn't been dramatically impactful." The company's processes were simply not sufficiently homogeneous or standardized to be amenable to today's AI competencies.

"We're at the infancy of what AI and ML can bring to the insurance industry," another leader observed. "We're tinkering . . . just scratching the surface of how AI and ML are capable of disrupting the industry." Moreover, the challenges are business and organizational. "It's not about the technology" but rather about the ability of the firm to crystallize its problems in a way that they are solvable by even today's technology. "We lack the maturity [as an industry] in coming up with what's possible."

Consider one example where a firm successfully implemented an AI-based system: creating efficiency in evaluating legal bills. As an insurance company, this firm hires thousands of law firms over a broad area of states and jurisdictions, and the company must audit the legal bills to be sure the charges comply with the company's policies. It buys more than a billion dollars' worth of legal services annually and employs a couple of dozen auditors—college-educated attorneys and financial specialists who read through the bills to verify the claims.

Applying AI to this problem required convening three separate groups of experts: data scientists who understood the electronic billing formats, coders who wrote algorithms, and auditors, who initially resisted the idea. It took months of learning, coordination, and development to build machine learning models to calibrate algorithms to detect anomalies in bills. After a few cycles of trial, including presentation to and support from the CEO, the model achieved 85 percent accuracy. When the models were applied to the end of the auditing process, the results persuaded the auditors that the algorithms could pick up anomalies that the humans had missed. Soon the system was yielding millions of dollars in annual savings, freeing the auditors to move on to more complex work. This AI system has had a substantial impact, though it proceeded much as a traditional IT project, requiring the right mix of experts, innovative teamwork, executive support, and upfront investment before showing benefits.

Reynolds and her team found that AI-based software systems did not result in laying off entire teams of people, but they did slow down hiring in relevant departments, as in the earlier example. While both layoffs and hiring slowdowns ultimately mean fewer employees in the affected departments, they have qualitatively different effects on workers.

This company still relies on the traditional role of the insurance agent. Here, AI and RPA have largely been complementary. Insurance, like other retail products, is now sold through an omnichannel approach: direct to consumer (online), direct response center (online plus human on the phone, or just the latter), and in person. This situation is likely to change as the next generation of customers becomes more comfortable engaging the company without human assistance.

Ten years ago, the firm expected to see in-person agent jobs fade away and more direct-to-consumer activity. But despite pickup in the latter arena, the number of in-person agents has remained relatively constant. Customers still want human interactions before they purchase insurance. While used by only a fraction of customers, self-service options let agents spend more time selling insurance to those who want in-person interactions, increasing their sales and commissions and allowing for more customized insurance packages. At the same time, new digital technologies like e-signatures are making certain tasks more efficient by obviating the signing of stacks of documents. Machine learning algorithms provide more insight into existing or potential customers through the collection, aggregation, and analysis of third-party data. These data enable predictions that a customer might be calling about an upcoming bill; they can suggest calling the family to offer adding a new driver to the auto policy because a child has just turned sixteen. While agents have had to become more technologically savvy with the use of apps and tablets, the new training required is modest and acquired on the job.

In another industry example, heavy investment in new tools and technologies in health care is yielding rapid change. The Task Force's John Van Reenen and the MIT Sloan School of Management's Joseph Doyle, working with PhD candidate Ari Bronsoler, took a close look at the impact of this technology, including electronic medical records, on the sector.[8]

Health care is a potential bright spot for workers in low- and middle-paying jobs, though this doesn't apply to the rapidly growing realm of home health delivery. The good news is that health care jobs of all kinds favor human labor for the foreseeable future. Health care employment is 11 percent of US employment and growing rapidly, which appears likely to continue as the population ages and new treatments emerge. It is also a sector that offers good jobs, with reasonable wage and nonwage benefits, at least for those working directly for health care systems. By contrast, home health care workers are poorly paid with few benefits.[9]

The sector is also considered to be recession-proof; though, ironically, the COVID-19 crisis caused a steep fall in health care employment as people chose to avoid elective medical procedures and doctors' offices during the pandemic.[10]

Bronsoler, Doyle, and Van Reenen conclude that the rise of new technologies in health care has the potential to slow the growth of new jobs but not to reduce the overall number of jobs. At the same time, new technology is clearly altering the mix of workers you might see in a hospital. Workers who specialize in the use of computer applications outpaced nurses in both employment and wage growth in recent years (see figure 3.1).

Still, for all of the new health care technology and investment in IT, the sector has, surprisingly, shown relatively little productivity growth. Lessons from other industries suggest that the management of new technologies is an important driver of productivity gains.[11] This poses particular challenges for an industry renowned for being highly fragmented, with clinical workers used to a high degree of autonomy when it comes

Employment share in US workforce

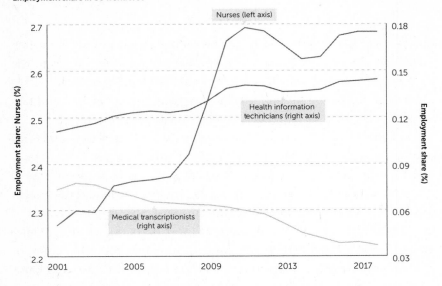

Average hourly wages relative to US mean

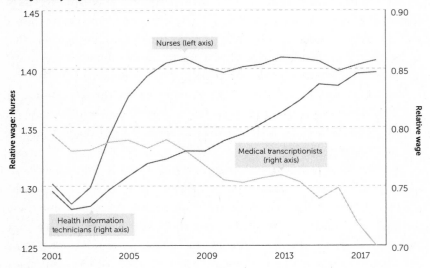

Figure 3.1

Employment and Earnings of Nurses, Medical Transcriptionists, and Health Information Technicians, 2001–2018. Upper panel reports the employment of nurses, medical transcriptionists, and health care information technicians as a share of the total US workforce. Lower panel reports the average hourly rates of nurses, medical transcriptionists, and health care information technicians relative to the mean hourly wage in the US economy. Figures are based on Occupational Employment Statistics data provided by the US Bureau of Labor Statistics (http://www.bls.gov.oes/tables.htm).

to making choices about patients. "Despite the presence of so much technology in health care," one senior health care technology leader interviewed during the course of this research acknowledged, "it's hard to bring it together and use it to its full effect."

New electronic health record (EHR) technology such as Epic is the most significant IT investment in health care in decades, with $30 billion dedicated to its implementation since 2010. The rapid adoption of EHR technology was spurred by the 2009 Health Information Technology for Economic and Clinical Health (HITECH) Act, part of the Affordable Care Act, which aims to increase the use of EHRs. EHRs serve as a platform for decision support, combining patient-level data with best practices and clinical guidelines, as well as data analytics that can lead to larger long-term gains in quality and efficiency. Yet, for all the benefits and potential the technology brings to improving health care productivity, limitations remain, including a lack of robust competition in the EHR market, which can slow adoption and innovation. "Epic was designed for the health care of the past and built on the health care of the past," said one senior health care IT expert, "not for the health care at the digital frontier."

As in other industries, new technologies used by those directly employed by health care systems tend to complement the work of highly educated and highly specialized workers, and to substitute for workers with less specialized expertise. On the clinical side, AI and machine learning technologies are driving significant change through the use of medical imaging to read radiographs, natural language processing to read clinical documentation, and data science to process massive amounts of data to generate inferences and predictions about patient diagnoses. These technologies tend to provide greater insights for clinicians as well as increased efficiency. New scanning technologies for nurses, for example, that allow nurses to scan every piece of information about a patient, including medications, rather than manually typing in information, lead to improved safety and efficiency. Likewise, new communication technologies, such as secure messaging rather than pager technology, allow nurses to reach other team members (doctors, residents, other nurses) in a timely manner to discuss treatment protocols and ensure the consistency, accuracy, and timeliness of treatment. In both these cases, the technology is complementing a subset of tasks while replacing others. Amid these many technological changes, the wages of nurses as compared to those of average US workers have remained relatively constant over the past fifteen years (while rising for health IT workers—see figure 3.1).

New technologies hold the potential for large cost savings in health care. A well-known RAND study estimated that adoption of digital technologies could save between $142 billion and $371 billion over a fifteen-year period.[12] So far, the actual results of the impact of the HITECH Act have been disappointing. A subsequent RAND study by Kellerman and Jones found that the predicted savings had not materialized, in part because of a lack of information sharing across providers and a lack of acceptance by the workforce in an environment where incentives run counter to the goal of reducing health care costs.[13] When it comes to the impact of new technologies on cost savings, the much greater focus for health care systems is on nonclinical work. This includes back-office and clerical work such as finance, administration, compliance, billing, health information, and supply chain management. In interviews at a large health care system, senior technology leaders outlined their goal of reducing their labor dependency with automation. One senior executive estimated that 50 to 60 percent of human resource work could be replaced by RPA. The challenge, however, is a familiar one—how to align processes such that they can be easily automated. There is little uniformity on how tasks are performed: "There are thirteen different ways of doing things because there are thirteen different departments," the executive confirmed. "The challenge is the ability to change the culture within an organization to do things in a particular way."

In the case of one large health care system, RPA has been introduced to replace multiple tasks, from the classic scanning of medical records to verifying clinicians' licenses and rapidly communicating details about drug recalls across a hospital. However, one senior leader emphasized that automation has not led to one-for-one replacement of a worker. In most cases, the tasks that have been automated represent a modest subset of the tasks in which the worker is engaged. Typically, workers have been redeployed or have found different jobs within the system, in part because the health care system as a whole has been growing in recent years. As suggested earlier, the primary impact on jobs has been the elimination of open positions (retirements have also played a role in the transition), which in the long run implies a decline in employment in those positions.

Not all transitions have been painless, however. Employees with non-transferable skills, such as medical transcriptionists, have been hit hard as their relative employment and wages have fallen steadily since the early 2000s. According to HR leaders, it has been challenging to place these workers in new positions within the organization, and many have been let go since the introduction of EHRs. Some recent studies conclude that every position in health care based on paperwork will eventually become obsolete, although there may be much work remaining in the nonpaper-work versions of those activities.[14]

The introduction of health care IT tends to be associated with an increase in costs, as Bronsoler, Doyle, and Van Reenen discuss, but it has had a positive impact on patient outcomes. One can anticipate with rea-sonable (but far from complete) confidence that the former will tend to decrease while the latter will continue to grow. Health care IT will likely be adopted at an increasing rate. The impact on the workforce, as in other industries, appears likely to be a steady increase in the need for technical skills, whether working on the front lines or in the back office.

THE ROBOTS YOU CAN SEE: DRIVERLESS CARS, WAREHOUSING AND DISTRIBUTION, AND MANUFACTURING

Few sectors better illustrate the promises and fears of robotics than auton-omous cars and trucks. Autonomous vehicles (AVs) are essentially high-speed wheeled industrial robots powered by cutting-edge technologies of perception, machine learning, decision-making, regulation, and user interfaces. Their cultural and symbolic resonance has brought AVs to the forefront of excited press coverage about new technology and has sparked large investments of capital, making a potentially "driverless" future a focal point for hopes and fears of a new era of automation.

The ability to transport goods and people across the landscape under computer control embodies a dream of twenty-first-century technol-ogy, and also the potential for massive social change and displacement. In a driverless future, accidents and fatalities could drop significantly. The time that people waste stuck in traffic could be recovered for work or leisure. Urban landscapes might change, requiring less parking and improving safety and efficiency for all. New models for the distribution of goods and services promise a world where people and objects move effortlessly through the physical world, much as bits move effortlessly through the internet.

As recently as a decade ago, it was common to dismiss the notion of driverless cars coming to roads in any form. Federally supported university research in robotics and autonomy had evolved for two generations and had just begun to yield advances in military robotics. Yet today, virtually every carmaker in the world, plus many startups, have engaged to redefine mobility. The implications for job disruption are massive. The auto industry itself accounts for just over 5 percent of all private sector jobs, according to one estimate. Millions more work as drivers and in the web of companies that service and maintain these vehicles.

Task Force members John J. Leonard and David A. Mindell have both participated in the development of these technologies and, with graduate student Erik L. Stayton, have studied their implications. Their research suggests that the grand visions of automation in mobility will not be fully realized in the space of a few years.[15] The variability and complexity of real-world driving conditions require the ability to adapt to unexpected situations that current technologies have not yet mastered. The recent tragedies and scandals surrounding the death of 346 people in two Boeing 737 MAX crashes stemming from flawed software and the accidents involving self-driving car-testing programs on public roads have increased public and regulatory scrutiny, adding caution about how quickly these technologies will be widely dispersed. The software in driverless cars remains more complex and less deterministic than that in airliners; we still lack technology and techniques to certify it as safe. Some even argue that solving for generalized autonomous driving is tantamount to solving for AGI.

Analysis of the best available data suggests that the reshaping of mobility around autonomy will take more than a decade and will proceed in phases, beginning with systems limited to specific geographies such as urban or campus shuttles (such as the recent product announcement from Zoox, an American AV company). Trucking and delivery are also likely use cases for early adoption, and several leading developers are focusing on these applications both in a fully autonomous mode and as augmented, "convoy" systems led by human drivers. In late 2020, in a telling shift for the industry from "robotaxis" to logistics, Uber sold its driverless car unit, having spent billions of dollars with few results. The unit was bought by Amazon-backed Aurora to focus the technology on trucking. More automated systems will eventually spread as technological barriers are overcome, but current fears about a rapid elimination of driving jobs are not supported.

AVs, whether cars, trucks, or buses, combine the industrial heritage of Detroit and the millennial optimism and disruption of Silicon Valley with a DARPA-inspired military vision of unmanned weapons. Truck drivers, bus drivers, taxi drivers, auto mechanics, and insurance adjusters are but a few of the workers expected to be displaced or complemented. This transformation will come in conjunction with a shift toward full electric technology, which would also eliminate some jobs while creating others.[16] Electric cars require fewer parts than conventional cars, for instance, and the shift to electric vehicles will reduce work supplying motors, transmissions, fuel injection systems, pollution control systems, and the like. This change too will create new demands, such as for large-scale battery production (that said, the power-hungry sensors and computing of AVs will at least partially offset the efficiency gains of electric cars). AVs may well emerge as part of an evolving mobility ecosystem as a variety of innovations, including connected cars, new mobility business models, and innovations in urban transit, converge to reshape how we move people and goods from place to place.

TRANSPORTATION JOBS IN A DRIVERLESS WORLD

The narrative on AVs suggests the replacement of human drivers by AI-based software systems, themselves created by a few PhD computer scientists in a lab. This is, however, a simplistic reading of the technological transition currently under way, as MIT researchers discovered through their work in Detroit. It is true that AV development organizations tend to have a higher share of workers with advanced degrees compared to the traditional auto industry. Even so, implementation of AV systems requires efforts at all levels, from automation supervision by safety drivers to remote managing and dispatching to customer service and maintenance roles on the ground.

Take, for instance, a current job description for "site supervisor" at a major AV developer. The job responsibilities entail overseeing a team of safety drivers focused in particular on customer satisfaction and reporting feedback on mechanical and vehicle-related issues. The job offers a mid-range salary with benefits, does not require a two- or four-year degree, but does require at least one year of leadership experience and communication skills. Similarly, despite the highly sophisticated machine learning and computer vision algorithms, AV systems rely on technicians routinely calibrating and cleaning various sensors both on the vehicle and in the built environment. The job description for field autonomy technician to maintain AV systems provides a mid-range salary, does not require a four-year degree, and generally requires only background knowledge of vehicle repair and electronics. Some responsibilities are necessary for implementation—including inventorying and budgeting repair parts and hands-on physical work—but not engineering.

The scaling up of AV systems, when it happens, will create many more such jobs, and others devoted to ensuring safety and reliability. Simultaneously, an AV future will require explicit strategies to enable workers displaced from traditional driving roles to transition to secure employment.

A rapid emergence of AVs would be highly disruptive for workers since the US has more than three million commercial vehicle drivers. These drivers are often people with high school or lower education or immigrants with language barriers. Leonard, Mindell, and Stayton conclude that a slower adoption timeline will ease the impact on workers, enabling current drivers to retire and younger workers to get trained to fill newly created roles, such as monitoring mobile fleets.[17] Again, realistic adoption timelines provide opportunities for shaping technology, adoption, and policy. A 2018 report by Task Force Research Advisory Board member Susan Helper and colleagues discusses a range of plausible scenarios and found the employment impact of AVs to be proportional to the time to widespread adoption. Immediate, sudden automation of the fleet would, of course, put millions out of work, whereas a thirty-year adoption timeline could be accommodated by retirements and generational change.[18]

Meanwhile, car- and truck makers already make vehicles that augment rather than replace drivers. These products include high-powered cruise control and warning systems frequently found on vehicles sold today. At some level, replacement-type driverless cars will be competing with augmentation-type computer-assisted human drivers. In aviation, this competition went on for decades before unmanned aircraft found their niches, while human-piloted aircraft became highly augmented by automation. When they did arrive, unmanned aircraft such as the US Air Force's Predator and Reaper vehicles required many more people to operate than traditional aircraft and offered completely novel capabilities, such as persistent, twenty-four-hour surveillance.[19]

Based on the current state of knowledge, we estimate a slow shift toward systems that require no driver, even in trucking, one of the easier use cases, with limited use by 2030. Overall shifts in other modes, including passenger cars, are likely to be no faster.

Even when it's achieved, a future of AVs will not be jobless. New business models, potentially entirely new industrial sectors, will be spurred by the technology. New roles and specialties will appear in expert, technical fields of engineering of AV systems and vehicle information technologies. Automation supervision or safety driver roles will be critical for levels of automation that will come before fully automated driving. Remote management or dispatcher, roles will bring drivers into control rooms and require new skills of interacting with automation. New customer service, field support technician, and maintenance roles will also appear. Perhaps most important, creative use of the technology will enable new businesses and services that are difficult to imagine today. When passenger cars displaced equestrian travel and the myriad occupations that supported it in the 1920s, the roadside motel and fast-food industries rose up to serve the "motoring public." How will changes in mobility, for example, enable and shape changes in distribution and consumption?

Equally important are the implications of new technologies for how people get to work. As with other new technologies, introducing expensive new autonomous cars into existing mobility ecosystems will just perpetuate existing inequalities of access and opportunity if institutions that support workers don't evolve as well. In a sweeping study of work, inequality, and transit in the Detroit region, Task Force researchers noted that most workers building Model T and Model A Fords on the early assembly lines traveled to work on streetcars, using Detroit's then highly developed system.[20] In the century since, particularly in Detroit, but also in cities all across the country, public transit has been an essential service for many workers, but it has also been an instrument facilitating institutional racism, urban flight to job-rich suburbs, and inequality. Public discourse and political decisions favoring highway construction often denigrated and undermined mass transit, with racial undertones. As a result, Black people and other minorities are much more likely to lack access to personal vehicles.

"Technology alone cannot remedy the mobility constraints" that workers face, the study concludes, "and will perpetuate existing inequities absent institutional change." As with other technologies, deploying new technologies in old systems of transportation will exacerbate their inequalities by "shifting attention toward what is new and away from what is useful, practical, and needed." Innovating in institutions is as important as innovating in machines; recent decades have seen encouraging pilot programs, but more must be done to scale those pilots to broader use and ensure accountability to the communities they intend to serve. "Transportation offers a unique site of political possibility."[21]

WAREHOUSING AND DISTRIBUTION

Technologies often have their greatest impact, and create the most jobs, when they enable new business models and transform industries, rather than automating tasks previously done by people. The rise of e-commerce, whereby the internet has enabled entirely new ways of shopping and ordering for consumers and businesses, epitomizes such a transformation, especially through its impact on the movement and distribution of goods ("logistics").

E-commerce can be seen as a kind of automation of retail shopping, with corresponding employment effects in the retail sector. Whereas a customer used to have to visit a store to select, purchase, and carry home a product, now the consumer can use a web page to enter an order directly into a semi-automated supply chain, with the delivery accomplished by a mix of people and machines.

Within a four-decade adoption cycle, the greatest impact of technology on logistics and warehousing is perhaps only partway through this forty-year cycle. IT and networking are still transforming the system.

As with mobility, news reports on distribution might lead one to believe that jobs are about to start drying up. Indeed, a Google search for "warehouse automation" produces 73 million hits, many of them promotions for new systems, suggesting a rapidly changing landscape. The landscape is unquestionably rich with exciting new technology and investment.[22]

But Task Force member Frank Levy, working with Wellesley College student Arshia Mehta, found a gradual process of adoption under way. They queried automation suppliers, distribution center managers, and leaders in established companies and startups.[23] One-third of respondents to a recent published survey reported using automated guided vehicles but less than one-fifth reported using automated packaging solutions, collaborative robotics, or automated picking.[24]

Compared to other industries, logistics is geographically dispersed, and present in more rural areas. We define logistics as the sum of three industries: warehousing and storage, freight trucking, and freight trucking arrangements (i.e., brokers and third-party logistics providers, or 3PLs), accounting for just over three million jobs (before the COVID-19 pandemic struck). This amounts to about 2 percent of jobs in the economy (about one-fourth the size of manufacturing).

E-commerce has driven two fundamental changes in logistics. First, the industry has historically been set up for the delivery of goods in bulk sizes to local retailers for sale. E-commerce has changed the endpoint for the bulk of those deliveries from warehouses and distribution centers to individual residences. Second, e-commerce has radically reduced the size of orders that logistics centers must now handle, right down to individual items. The warehouse industry was traditionally built to handle the bulk movement of goods. Trucks would line up at rows of doors to disgorge products, which would then get reshuffled and dispatched again in large quantities to stores, restaurants, or other warehouses for further processing. But with e-commerce, warehouses now are just as likely to handle huge numbers of individual or small-batch items—a single toy ordered by a customer in California, for example, or a half dozen bottles of hand sanitizer ordered by a doctor's office in Connecticut.

Mehta and Levy argue that if we think of logistics employment as a tug-of-war between job gains from e-commerce and job losses from automation, job gains are winning decisively at present.[25] Since 2000, the trucking industry has added 130,000 jobs (to 1.75 million). The warehousing and storage industries have more than doubled, to 1.1 million, during that same period (about 30 percent of these are low-wage manual labor jobs). More of these gains were in rural rather than urban areas.

By some measures, productivity has not improved despite this vast expansion. Industry statistics find that productivity rose more than 20 percent from 2000 to 2014 but actually declined thereafter, leaving it less productive in 2019 than in 2000. A plausible explanation for this reversal is that the challenge of logistics has increased in the e-commerce era.[26] Today, distribution and fulfillment centers face the problem of unloading, unwrapping, storing, accurately selecting ("picking"), and packing products, from small jewelry to fifty-pound bags of pet food and large sports equipment.

Warehouses have been slow to adopt automation; their rapid output increases from 2014 to 2019 were achieved by adding labor in less automated facilities. Many of these tasks—in particular, picking and packing individual items ("each picks")—are still performed by people. The simple challenge of removing plastic wrapping from a pallet of goods remains beyond today's commercially available robots.

"In warehousing," Mehta and Levy write, "robotic arms that can identify, grasp, and manipulate streams of diverse items are still in their infancy." Great effort and investment is going into automated gripping systems, but it will take an estimated three to five years to develop the technologies that would endanger the numerous jobs in picking and packing.[27] This time frame, however, does not account for the extended time for broad diffusion, as retrofitting older warehouses and fulfillment centers with state-of-the-art technology is a disruptive and risky investment (some industry leaders we spoke to saw the timeline for automated picking pushed out further still). Today, humanlike physical dexterity, including its wondrous flexibility, remains out of reach for robotic systems.

As elsewhere, major impacts on labor and efficiency are coming from maturing applications of decades-old IT. What gains in efficiency there have been in trucking have come from the "arrangements" sector, where digital tools improve such processes as brokering, loading, and scheduling. "Significant technology," write Mehta and Levy, "is not always the newest technology."

Thirty years ago, an employee in a truck brokerage connected firms to truckers using a Rolodex, a telephone, personal relationships, and a fax machine. The connection process began when a firm called a broker with the details of a shipping job, including what it wanted to pay (subject to negotiation). In making the connection, the size of the broker's Rolodex was key. A large set of contacts meant the broker might be able to offer a trucker a sequence of shipments with little time when the truck was driving empty.

Third-party logistics firms operated in a similar way, with one important addition: the need to plan an efficient route in which a trucker delivered shipments from several firms to several different destinations. By the end of the 1980s, 3PLs were using computerized spreadsheets (e.g., Lotus 1-2-3) to help in trial-and-error route design.

Because brokers and 3PLs deal in information, the evolution of digital tools has sharply increased what employees can do and how they do it. For the traditional broker, a connection no longer begins with a phone call from a firm with a shipping job. Instead, many firms now post jobs directly on large, digital job boards. A broker surveys one or more boards to find jobs for which they think they have a potential driver. Being able to view many jobs at once increases the chances of constructing a trip with limited time spent driving empty.

Some startups are expanding the self-service aspect of the digital job board by encouraging drivers to use proprietary mobile phone applications to access their job board directly. In a few cases, a startup can use machine learning to identify the kinds of jobs a trucker prefers and alert the trucker when such jobs appear. While humans are still needed to deal with problems that might arise—for example, a scheduled shipment that isn't ready to be picked up—these startups are trying to automate broker jobs, much as the direct purchase of airline tickets has automated travel agent jobs.

At the same time, digitalization allows brokers and 3PLs to automate highly routine tasks that were previously performed by lower-level employees. In some cases in which a 3PL has a steady relationship with a firm, it can offer a self-service ordering portal where a firm can specify all aspects of a shipment—the type and shape of containers, precise pick-up and drop-off locations, the presence of any hazardous materials, and so on. Previously, this information might have been collected in a back-and-forth exchange with a person. Shipping documents that used to be hand collected from the web (e.g., a signed proof of delivery) are now scraped off the web automatically.

As a result, the employment mix, particularly in 3PLs, has shifted away from hourly personnel to salaried personnel with training in software design, data analysis, and related fields. Similarly, the technologies transforming most warehouses are not robots at all but IT, often known as "warehouse management systems." These software systems record and track products from loading dock to loading dock and connect to other systems that track the supply chain.

Many fewer warehouses use robotic systems. A 2019 survey conducted by the Modern Materials Handling Institute confirmed that while 80 percent of survey respondents used warehouse management systems and 86 percent used bar code scanners, only 26 percent used even the mature technology of radio-frequency identification (RFID) tags. With respect to automated goods movement, 63 percent used conveyor and sortation systems, but only 22 percent used automated storage and retrieval systems, and 15 percent used autonomous mobile robots. Robotics and automation, especially when combined with IT innovations, are rapidly evolving and taking novel forms. Automated storage and retrieval systems (ASRS) resemble automated warehouses in a box, though they remain expensive and suitable for only the largest high-throughput applications. In Amazon's Kiva robot system, armies of mobile robots carry shelves of randomly mixed items to human pickers, forming a kind of distributed ASRS. Elsewhere in "Pick to light" systems, computer-controlled lights guide human pickers to select items. Robotic carts (such as those made by 6 River Systems, recently acquired by Shopify) accompany human pickers through aisles and help them rapidly pick orders. Various forms of automated forklifts and tuggers are finding niche applications and will surely grow in robustness and flexibility.

"What I would really like is software that keeps track of every person and every robot on the floor and tells each of them what it should do next," one manager told Mehta and Levy. Such systems exist today. But they are complex and extremely difficult to develop and deploy, especially in a rapidly changing industry that is simply struggling to keep up with demand. They also raise concerns about surveillance. One can imagine an evolution toward a world in which an entire fulfillment or distribution center, or even an entire supply chain, becomes a collaborative robotic system comprising people, robots, and infrastructure, all quickly reconfigurable with software. How can such systems develop to value human autonomy and flexibility, without simply treating workers like software-directed automata?

As in manufacturing, higher levels of automation are most viable for large firms.

The largest warehouse firms gain a potentially large cost advantage because they have the resources to afford the risk and expense required to implement advanced automation. Smaller firms often pursue automation investment incrementally; leasing robots is finding some success as a business model because it enables smaller firms to apply robots without capital expense in a rapidly changing industry.

Outside the warehouse, the logistics industry stands to benefit from the advancing capabilities of autonomous vehicles described above. As in other AV arenas, the path remains long and the direction uncertain. We described the AV potential in long-haul trucking. But even if the driverless truck problem were perfectly solved today, the time constant for change would be half a generation. The typical Class 8 truck (over 33,000 pounds) stays on the road an average of fourteen years before it is junked (though it might be retired sooner were sufficiently better technology to come along). Automated platooning, with a single human driver leading several following unmanned vehicles, is likely coming sooner, though the labor impacts are more incremental. As with other types of robots, autonomous trucks are likely to benefit larger, better-capitalized fleets, such as J. B. Hunt's, and corporate fleets, such as those of UPS and Walmart.

Much of the employment growth in e-commerce trucking has been in the last few miles of local delivery. Techie publications abound with images of mini-delivery robots plying urban streets or delivery drones conveying much-needed medicines to rural areas. The possibilities are indeed compelling and the technologies exciting (potentially more so in the COVID-19 era). Current demonstrations of these delivery robots are often monitored by human operators with backup radio control. The promise is that these operators, like the safety drivers in autonomous cars and trucks, will be removed at some point in the future, or will supervise large fleets of vehicles. But the complexity of the environment, including curbs, pets, and noncooperative (i.e., ordinary) pedestrians to be avoided or navigated around, suggests that for some time it will be hard to achieve autonomous operation outside of constrained and well-defined areas.

Mehta and Levy conclude that fully autonomous trucks are not likely to displace significant numbers of truck drivers for at least a decade. During that time, warehouses will likely be dominated by low-wage jobs, some of which are at risk from increasing automation in picking and packing. Automation and robotics will create jobs for technicians, software developers, data scientists, and similarly skilled positions, but they will likely eliminate a larger number of picker and packer jobs in warehousing and driver jobs in trucking. "The occupational structure of freight transportation arrangements [brokers and 3PLs]," Mehta and Levy note, "already favors skilled positions, and continued automation of routine clerical tasks will further tilt the balance." As elsewhere, the development of new technologies will favor large firms and middle- and higher-skilled workers.

LIGHTS OUT FACTORIES? OR LIGHTS DIMMED?

The current state of the art in manufacturing parallels that in AVs—promising technologies abound, but the crucial work of making them robust and reliable poses myriad challenges.

As part of the Task Force's research, MIT robotics professor Julie Shah and her students studied the deployment of industrial robots in Germany, one arm of "Industry 4.0" efforts under way across Europe. Industry 4.0, which began as a strategic initiative in Germany in 2011, bills itself as the "fourth industrial revolution."

Its goal is to knit together machines and processes in factories so they can be monitored and controlled through advanced digital tools. Shah and her team assessed which technologies had been developed by researchers and adopted by industry, the challenges developers faced, which future paths companies deemed important, and the research challenges that remain for robotics to be widely adopted by industry. They found sizable gaps between technology's potential, even when demonstrated in research settings, and its actual use on shop floors today.[28]

Shah and her team looked at "top-down" approaches to automation—where the tasks are adapted to the technology—and "bottom-up" approaches, where workers start with tasks to be done and adapt technology accordingly. Generally, bottom-up approaches appear more successful, as the solutions are closer to the people and the tasks in need of improvement. One company set up robotic experience centers on the factory floor where engineers, working closely with line workers, could generate new ideas, prototype solutions, and make changes to production lines. Companies preferred "programming the task, and not the robot"—that is, solving a larger job to be done, and empowering people to guide the deployment of robots to raise productivity and address "pain points." As other Task Force studies have shown, worker voice remains an important component of success with today's automation.

Challenges remain in integrating robotics into manufacturing lines. Industrial robots have been at work in large-scale applications for decades, but most remain dangerous to people around them. Innovation in safety systems allows robotic systems to work more closely with people. Collaborative robot arms are one approach to this problem—they carry lighter payloads, run at slower speeds, and have other characteristics that make them acceptable to work outside cages. Their low cost also offers lower barriers to experimentation and deployment. However, to ensure safety, collaborative robots function at slower speeds and with less mechanical force than caged robots, which reduces their output and range of capabilities.

Rethinking production systems to combine IT with operations technology (OT) and generate vast amounts of real-time data creates challenges that are as much cognitive, social, and organizational as they are technical.

But even as the cost of robots is coming down, the human labor of integrating them into existing lines remains expensive. Efforts are under way to ease the transitions with better interfaces and easier programming, though the work remains hampered by a lack of standards and the high levels of human skill required to do the integrations. In fact, the adoption of the industrial "internet of things" (IoT)—low-cost ubiquitous sensor networks—has been slow, mostly because of data and security concerns and unclear value. Digital twins (computer models representing physical objects), advanced simulation, and augmented and virtual reality systems all remain promising colors in future automation palettes, but broad adoption requires overcoming similar challenges.

Technological bottlenecks also remain: in vision, perception and sensing, and robustness and reliability. "Deep learning-based approaches," for example, "haven't delivered well on their promise within industrial environments."[29] Such techniques require vast amounts of data, which is hard to come by in factories; they tend to be brittle and difficult to adapt to new situations, and sensitive to their original data sources as well as variations in the environment.

Autonomous guided vehicles (AGVs) have had an impact in industry in materials handling (as in warehousing, discussed above). These mobile robots carry everything from small totes to large vehicles around a production environment. Future visions include production lines where the line itself is never fixed and merely consists of products on AGVs carried past various self-organizing workstations—which are themselves made up of AGVs and robotic arms. But this vision has yet to materialize, held back by, among other things, the inability of AGVs to navigate with the millimeter precision required for production operations.

Better interfaces that enable easier programming push the applications of robotic systems closer to production lines, increasing flexibility and reducing costs. But because robotic systems remain difficult and expensive to program, Shah's team found that they largely remain technological islands on factory floors, not part of integrated digital oceans powered by AI. The researchers concluded that these technologies—even in Germany, where they are deeply rooted—"have yet to permeate the industrial landscape."

Shah also found a bottleneck identified in other Task Force studies: inadequate robotic dexterity. Until recently, robots used traditional forms of two-fingered pincers or single-purpose tools that can pick up objects but risk damaging soft or inconsistent materials. More recently, purpose-built automated grippers directed by machine vision can do remarkably delicate and precise work, such as picking up glazed donuts on an automated bakery line without cracking the shiny coating. But such a gripper might work only on doughnuts. It can't pick up a clump of asparagus or a car tire.

Today's gripping systems are evolving rapidly toward enabling robotic hands to grasp an ever-greater variety of products and parts. The search remains for a general-purpose gripper that could pick up any product in any orientation. Deep learning and other AI techniques have helped here (and they are making an impact in the logistics industry). Still, despite investment and confident predictions, most AI techniques remain too brittle, too complex, or too slow, for manufacturing operations. The generalized robotic dexterity problem may, like driving, be another example of the search for AGI. Major players in manufacturing and distribution have told us they believe that this problem is a decade or more away from resolution.

These findings largely resonate with the conclusions of a team of MIT researchers led by Task Force Research Advisory Board member Susan Helper. Helper and colleagues interviewed many US-based large firms, primarily automotive companies and their tier 1 (major) suppliers.[30] The research concentrated on the automotive industry because about 40 percent of all robots in the US (and globally) are found in this industry.[31] While firms in this sector are striving to move toward a more data-intensive and analytic form of manufacturing, information often remains siloed within firms, as well as between firms and their suppliers. Unlike earlier paradigms of mass production or lean production, the Industry 4.0 era remains in experimental and pilot stages, without yet a "coherent repeatable set of organizational practices or artifacts demonstrating substantial improvements in productivity."[32] Industry 4.0 technologies, the researchers observed, appear primarily as "add-ons to already existing practices rather than a comprehensive overhaul of production systems" often beginning with the identification of "pain points" in production systems and building from there.

Nevertheless, significant changes are afoot. Firms are experimenting with technologies and production systems that will flexibly adapt, whether they are making traditional vehicles or those that incorporate more electric or autonomous capabilities, or using additive manufacturing for new parts. Overall, digitization efforts aim to increase efficiencies along the course of the manufacturing cycle—from upstream design phases to the shop floor itself—and to reduce waste at each point along that cycle. Because of the uncertainty regarding these markets, firms are emphasizing flexibility. Like Shah's findings in Germany, Helper's team found that workers are still central to firms' production processes. However, firms have different practices in how they use technologies that affect which technologies are substitutes for, or complements to, worker skills and which may be the subject of organizational tension. In one case, a firm's data scientists developed an algorithm to determine when cooling fans should be replaced; technicians were resistant to a protocol that called on them to follow the algorithm and eschew discretion. However, when the data predicted with 95 percent accuracy when the fans would need maintenance, the technicians accepted the technology and realized they didn't need to be "firefighting" as much. In other cases, firms have been adding or deepening problem-solving tasks for their shop floor workers. One company introduced a machine vision system that at first led to a dramatic spike in reported defects. Because of their experience and training in statistical process control, workers were able to quickly point out that many of the defects were false positives. Together with engineers, they determined how to relocate the vision system for better results.

Many firms said their ideal workforce would mesh the domain knowledge of their older, more experienced workers with the tech-savvy knowledge of their newer, younger workers. These firms are organizing teams and training around this goal. Some firms are devoting substantial resources to upskill their workforces and have developed granular, individually tailored training modules that help bring older workers up to speed and equip newer workers with domain-specific knowledge. These large firm differ greatly in how much they draw on external institutions (such as community colleges) for training.

Rethinking production systems to combine IT with OT and generate vast amounts of real-time data creates challenges that are as much cognitive, social, and organizational as they are technical. "The most complex thing isn't the equipment or technology, the most complex thing is what people value," said one manager of North American operations for a tier 1 supplier. "Our maintenance people love swooping in with their capes and fixing equipment. They'd say the job is to fix something, but I'd say a better job is to stop something from breaking!" Predictive analytics are being used to do just this. But implementing this seemingly common-sense idea is not straightforward. Supervisors may feel technicians are not working hard if they don't see them fixing urgent problems; technicians may worry about their job security if there are fewer urgent problems to fix. Firms need to adjust incentive systems to ensure workers value these efforts. Ultimately, decisions about how the data are used, interpreted, and shared all shape how workers fit into the factories of the future and whether jobs are deskilled or upskilled. As in every other aspect of this study, management practices prove crucial in shaping how technologies are adopted.

"SURPRISED TO FIND VERY FEW ROBOTS ANYWHERE": SMALL AND MEDIUM-SIZED FIRMS

Shah's research team focused on robot makers and relatively cutting-edge firms in Germany, while Helper's team focused on large, US-based automotive-related companies that had used robotics in manufacturing for many years. Task Force member Suzanne Berger led a team studying manufacturing in the US with a particular focus on small and mid-sized manufacturing firms. Berger, who led MIT's Production in the Innovation Economy study in 2013, drew on several decades of research in the US, China, Japan, and the EU.

Some US firms are well on the road to using advanced automation, including America's automotive factories and Amazon warehouses. But Berger's researchers found a sharp divide between the automation in some large companies and in small and medium-sized enterprises (SMEs).[33]

The team visited plants owned by forty-four US companies, ten of which were large multinationals and thirty-four of which were SMEs, in Ohio, Massachusetts, and Arizona. SMEs are companies with fewer than five hundred workers; they represent 98 percent of all manufacturing establishments in the US and employ 43 percent of the nation's manu-facturing workers. More than half the companies that the team studied had previously participated in the 2013 study, enabling some analysis of change over time.

Productivity growth in US manufacturing has been slow over the past decades in comparison with that in other advanced industrial countries. It has been even slower in manufacturing SMEs. If we want to accelerate growth, shift to "greener" production, or raise wages, the work of Berger's team underscores that we need to understand why, when, and how SMEs acquire new technologies and train their workers for new skills. The researchers asked each company about new technology adoption in the past five years, how they found the skills to operate the equipment, and what became of workers who used to do the job when the new technology was so radically different that it required new operators to perform the task.

"We had read the literature predicting a massive wave of robots replacing workers over a 5- to 10-year horizon," the team reported, "so we were surprised to find very few robots anywhere." The largest adopter of robots they found was an Ohio company they had first visited in 2010, which had subsequently been acquired by a Japanese company. It now had more than a hundred robots, while its workforce had more than doubled. In all the other Ohio SMEs they studied, the team found only a single robot purchased in the previous five years. In Massachusetts, one. In Arizona, three.

Equally telling were the reasons that managers at these SMEs gave to explain the robot scarcity. Several said they wished they could purchase robots but that the typical size of the orders they received rarely justified the purchase. SMEs are mostly high-mix, low-volume producers. Robots are still too inflexible to be switched at a reasonable cost from one task to another. As Shah reported, the price of a robot is only about one quarter of the total cost.[34] The rest is the cost of programming and integration into a work cell or process.

All the firms studied had, however, purchased new equipment or software over the same previous five years, including CNC machines, new welding technology, laser- and water-jet cutters, servo-press metal stamping machines, and sensors. They had also purchased computer-aided design (CAD), data analytics, and even blockchain software. They were capturing data on production processes, though, like the managers interviewed in large companies, the managers in SMEs said they did not know what to do with most of the data they collected.

Smaller firms tend to automate incrementally, adding a machine here or there, rather than installing whole new systems that are more expensive to buy and integrate. This approach minimizes disruptions for workers while generally increasing factory productivity.[35]

Often, technology acquisition means modifying existing machines with new hardware and software rather than purchasing new ones. This approach leads to a kind of layering of technology, with new equipment brought in to function alongside older equipment, some dating back to the 1940s. This may be one reason why acquiring new technology in SMEs has not typically led to layoffs. Older workers without the skills to work on the new equipment continue to work on the older machines while younger workers, who are excited about the newest technologies, may be unwilling to invest time in learning to operate older equipment. The companies the researchers visited both in 2013 and in 2019 had increased their number of workers over that time period, and no firms reported layoffs with the introduction of new technology.

Even for some of the larger firms interviewed, automation today is as much about improving quality as it is about saving labor. A Boston-based plant manager put the goal as not "lights out" but "lights dimmed"—moving away from people manipulating objects on assembly lines and toward people on the shop floor analyzing production statistics on screens—though the researchers note that the number of workers in that particular plant has declined by 50 percent in the past two decades.

New orders and new production demands from customers drive technology acquisition in SMEs. And new technology drives the search for new skills and training. When researchers asked managers what they were looking for in new hires, the most frequent response was "Someone who will show up on time and stay." Many managers were deeply skeptical about the value of formal workplace education in community colleges and other programs for jobs they wished to fill. It's only when advanced technology enters the shop that their search for skills begins. The "perfect hire" would be someone who had previously done the same job, but such a person is rarely available, at least at the wages the manager is willing to pay. So managers usually turn to younger or more enterprising workers they already employ and ask them if they can figure out how to use the new software or hardware. The workers often turn to online videos.

As one worker who learned online how to master a new set of CAD/ CAM software in order to work on a new CNC machine said, "Technology takes a step, then workers take a step forward, too. People grow with the software."

For all these reasons, a promising route both to productivity growth and to better jobs starts with aiding the adoption of advanced manufacturing technology in the SMEs. At present, the largest national programs that work with SMEs are the Manufacturing Extension Partnership (MEP), whose major focus has been on improving "lean" manufacturing practices, and the Manufacturing USA institutes, which support and diffuse applied R&D, working primarily with large manufacturing companies. New programs and policy levers can advance both technology adoption and skills in SMEs, which remain the critical backbone of US manufacturing.

Despite the twentieth-century rise in uniformity and mass production, manufacturing today remains a highly dynamic environment. Model changes, evolving technology, shifts in supply chains, even upheavals such as Brexit and COVID-19 all mean that twenty-first-century manufacturing operates within an environment of constant change, even for stable, highly standardized products. A rubber gasket that fits into a chassis one day may not fit the same way the next day when its supplier changes. Robotics and automation still do best when most variables are fixed and operations are highly standardized, while human workers remain key to adapting to changing conditions. New AI and machine learning–based approaches to robotics, new sensors and actuators, and new software are making these machines more flexible, but it remains early in a long evolution.

IMPORTANT TECHNOLOGY ON THE HORIZON: ADDITIVE MANUFACTURING

At the further end of the technology adoption cycle is additive manufacturing (AM), popularly known as 3D printing. 3D printer technology is advancing rapidly and could be the most disruptive manufacturing technology on the horizon. Using a single machine to craft a complex finished part has the potential to replace vast numbers of production jobs. Aerospace engineers now use 3D printers to make inspection tooling and auto parts, and other manufacturers make prototypes and fixtures on the machines. The machines are spreading, but their use remains limited and concentrated in large firms with well-funded internal technology budgets.

3D printing has generated a great deal of excitement in the past decade for its potential impacts on manufacturing and supply chains. While not traditionally considered part of robotics, 3D printers can be thought of as desktop robots that mix hardware, materials, and software to create objects in entirely new ways. These machines have found traction as consumer products for "makers," and have occasioned strong industrial interest as well. The ability to produce prototypes, parts, or even entirely new products at the place and time of use has far-reaching implications. The supply chain could become digital until the point of purchase or deployment. Production could be distributed into digital warehouses that produced parts on demand. Companies such as Mercedes-Benz already use this technology to print spare parts for legacy vehicles.

"Additive manufacturing" distinguishes the approach from "subtractive manufacturing," such as machining, in which material is subtracted by a cutting tool from raw stock such as a block of steel. In AM, material is laid down in small increments by a computer-controlled placement head. While familiar consumer desktop 3D printers can do this with colored plastic and small parts, today's AM machines range from the nanoscale to those capable of producing large structural or metal components, in materials ranging from high-precision polymers to aerospace-grade titanium.

The power of AM lies not only in the moment of fabrication itself but also in its reach far upstream into design and downstream into the supply chain. Where subtractive manufacturing must obey rules of cutting tools, AM upends the traditional trade-offs of cost and complexity, providing designers greater freedom in realizing complex shapes. It also opens the door to AI-enabled "generative design" techniques, whereby AI designs prototypes that AM builds and engineers test, prototypes that can optimize parts for cost, weight, or strength in entirely new ways. Experts expect AM to complement more than replace subtractive manufacturing, and also to have profound effects on how products are designed, manufactured, and brought to market.

"Realizing mass customization at scale," writes Task Force member John Hart, a leading expert in AM, "would be unthinkable were it not for the rapidity of converting digital information into a physical form through the use of AM." Hart and his team studied the spread of AM and concluded that it will eventually allow companies to shift effortlessly to supply changing needs.[36] AM can also open the way for new businesses that couldn't exist without the tool. Align Technology's Invisalign product, for example, makes custom orthodontic retainers based on scans of an individual patient's mouth.

Configurable production assets, including AM systems, may enable firms to respond quickly in periods of uncertainty to pivot their production activities if needed. During the COVID-19 pandemic, for example, AM firms were quick to leverage existing production infrastructure and pre-qualified medical-grade materials for the production of nasopharyngeal swabs. These swabs are vital for virus testing and were in drastically short supply early in the crisis. The project, initiated by faculty at Harvard and MIT, in collaboration with companies Desktop Metal, Formlabs, Carbon, and others, resulted in the production of millions of swabs per week within a few weeks of initiation.

Still, large-scale adoption of AM, and its attendant potential impact on jobs, is slowed by high (though falling) costs and a lack of common standards, which may take years to develop. AM-based systems still do not have the high speed or low cost required for the large-scale production that has developed over more than a century in subtractive manufacturing. Material properties of built-up parts can lack the predictability that subtractive techniques already deliver for critical components. Standards for AM design, testing, and materials are lacking. And, ironically in light of our discussion of job loss, the growth of the industry is currently limited by the need for specialized professionals trained in AM techniques. These limitations will all be addressed over time, from innovations in high-rate AM production equipment to new training pipelines.

So, as in other areas, we see the opportunity to apply smart training strategies to ease factory workers into emerging roles. Manufacturers will likely need smaller teams of workers, but those remaining will need specialized training to operate the new machines.

In Quinlan and Hart's study, the owner of one small Ohio plant predicted that he could transition entirely to the new technology in about a decade, and that it would result in many fewer jobs if his production volume stayed constant. But he also believed that he would grow so productive compared to his competitors that his own workforce would likely grow. Whether this means more industry jobs in net, or simply more jobs at this firm but fewer at its competitors, depends on how customer demand responds to improving quality and lower costs.[37]

MOMENTOUS IMPACTS, UNFOLDING GRADUALLY

Just as it took years to diffuse the major technological advances of earlier eras, such as interchangeable parts, assembly lines, and internet connectivity, it will take time to roll out today's advanced technologies throughout the economy. The most profound effects from the introduction of the internet, mobile and cloud computing, and other innovations dating back to the 1990s and earlier are still playing out. AI, machine learning, robotics, and AM are indeed poised to transform the economy, transformations that will be the culminations of thousands of innovations from managers, organizations, and business models.

4

EDUCATION AND TRAINING: PATHWAYS TO BETTER JOBS

Innovative technology has been changing the nature of work across industries and occupations. Indeed, as the previous chapter shows, the US has not lacked for innovation over the last four decades. Inventing ways of accomplishing existing work, new business models, and entirely new industries drives rising productivity and new jobs. But innovation in technology alone will not generate broadly shared gains absent complementary and reforms. It is equally important to invest in educating and training the country's workforce to ensure that workers have the skills and opportunities to fill jobs that are in demand. Training workers can also improve access to good jobs for workers who may face barriers to these jobs, and it can also help improve the quality of existing jobs by creating opportunities for career ladders. This chapter reviews the critical role education and training institutions play in creating and shaping the work of the future and highlights in particular innovative new approaches to skills development for adult workers.

Every society develops and supports its workforce through a web of institutions that reflects the social contract. In European countries, for example, that web is often tightly knit. Employers collaborate with one another and with governmental and educational institutions to train workers both in the classroom and through work-based learning.

Americans have often viewed the European model as rigid and costly. The US model, in contrast, is decentralized. State and federal agencies do little to coordinate workforce development efforts. Companies compete fiercely for skilled labor rather than banding together to develop it. These institutional features create a complex landscape of choices of uncertain quality for workers seeking training. At the same time, this arrangement facilitates competition and creative destruction and allows workers flexibility to move in and out of a diverse set of educational and training programs at different stages of life. Despite the decentralized nature of the US system, there is ample opportunity to build a more stable, supportive, and innovative workforce development system with the country's existing institutions. That it will likely retain much of the fragmented character of the current system does not prevent reform and strengthening of current institutions to better serve the majority of workers.

RETURNS ON EDUCATION AND TRAINING

While K–12 education is critical to the formation of an educated and productive workforce, we focus in this book on education and training for adults, particularly those whose jobs may be more vulnerable to automation. These workers typically (though not exclusively) include those in lower-wage jobs, those whose education pathways include alternatives to four-year degrees, and those who are displaced mid-career. Creating opportunities for these workers requires both investing in existing educational and training institutions and innovating to create new training mechanisms to make ongoing skills development accessible, engaging, and cost-effective.

The skills training system for adults is directly targeted at assisting workers in a changing labor market. This system includes employers, community colleges, unions, and public training programs. It also includes innovative new venues—both online and offline—that prepare workers for the job market. Within these categories, the quality of training varies widely, with correspondingly varying outcomes for workers. The system's heterogeneity and complexity have obvious downsides, but they also mean that US workers have multiple points at which to access training and education throughout adulthood. This flexibility is rare in more centralized European systems.

Before reviewing what we know about our current education and training system, it is worth reviewing what's happened in the labor market in recent decades with respect to returns to different levels of education.

As outlined briefly in chapter 2, the ongoing process of machine substitution for routine human labor complements the skills of educated workers who excel in abstract tasks that harness problem-solving ability, intuition, creativity, and persuasion—tasks that are at present difficult to automate but essential to perform. Simultaneously, it devalues the skills of workers, typically those without postsecondary education, who compete most directly with machinery in performing routine-intensive activities. The net effect of these forces is to further raise the demand for formal education, technical expertise, and cognitive ability.

In 1981, the average college graduate earned 48 percent more per week than the average high school graduate—a significant earnings gap but not an earnings gulf (see figure 2.2). The slowdown in college enrollment following the end of the Vietnam War meant a slowdown in new college graduates entering the labor market just a few years later, in the late 1970s and early 1980s. Because the demand for college graduates had been rising for decades, this slowdown generated a rapid rise in the market wages of college graduates, particularly among young college graduates, who were in the scarcest supply. This premium notched remarkably rapid year-over-year gains from 1982 forward, reaching 72 percent in 1990, 90 percent in 2000, and 97 percent in 2005.[1] Thus the average earnings of college graduates were 1.5 times those of high school graduates in 1982 but were double those of high school graduates by 2005. These differentials have been largely stable since that time.[2] Even accounting for the rising cost of college tuition, the expected net present value of a college degree relative to a high school diploma roughly tripled between 1965 and 2008 for both men and women, with the fastest gains accruing during the 1980s and 1990s.[3] One should, of course, be cautious in drawing cause-and-effect inferences from these descriptive statistics. Perhaps these earnings gaps reflect differences in the earnings potential of students who do and do not obtain college degrees rather than the added value of college degrees per se. Research has shown, however, that when near-identical students are admitted versus denied entry to college, there are large earnings returns for the students who go to college.[4]

The steep gains to four-year college degree attainment over the last four decades have not benefited workers with a two-year degree to nearly the same extent, as is seen in figure 2.2 (where they are labeled "Some college").[5] Nevertheless, workers with a non-BA college education have fared far better than either workers without a high school diploma or workers with high school diplomas but no college education. Moreover, a variety of evidence suggests that the gains from two-year degrees are sizable on average, especially relative to their low out-of-pocket cost and (comparatively) limited time investment.

When students complete a degree or certificate at a community college, the rate of return is generally favorable. While randomized controlled trials are not available for standard programs, sophisticated fixed effects modeling—sometimes using survey data and sometimes using administrative data—support this conclusion. For example, an assessment using administrative data from six states found that completing an associate of arts (AA) degree improved earnings by between $4,640 and $7,160 compared to entering the college and not obtaining the credential.[6] Smaller but positive results were also reported for completion of a certificate. A study of career and technical education (CTE) in California community colleges reported earnings gains of between 14 and 28 percent, and other studies have reached similar conclusions.[7]

Community college credentials are highly heterogeneous, of course, and may include two-year degrees, diplomas in various specialties, and certificates in specific skillsets.[8] This diversity of offerings gives rise to substantial heterogeneity in the returns on community college credentials. Ann Huff Stevens, Michal Kurlaender, and Michel Grosz estimate that the returns on CTE certificates and degrees range from 14 to 45 percent, with the largest returns seen for programs in the health care sector. For non-health-related programs, they estimate smaller returns, in the range of 15 to 23 percent.[9] These observations highlight that community college credentials do not for the most part correspond to so-called general skills training akin to a liberal arts education but rather to specific competencies for specific occupational opportunities. As such, the "return" on acquiring these credentials will depend heavily on the earnings level of the occupation to which these credentials provide entry. Since many specialized health-related occupations are relatively well remunerated, it is logical that health-related credentials tend to have high returns.

SECTORAL TRAINING PROGRAMS

One of the important models to emerge over several decades that directly address the mismatch between employer skill demands and workforce training is the sector-focused training program. Sector-focused training programs, also known as sectoral employment programs, train job seekers for high-quality employment in specific industries and occupational clusters. Sectors are chosen because of local labor market demand and long-term career prospects (e.g., health care, IT, manufacturing). The earliest sectoral employment programs emerged in the 1980s and were led by community-based organizations. Core elements of such programs can be found as part of a range of different training and education programs led by providers such as community colleges and labor market intermediaries. Significant and rigorous long-term evaluation of these programs gives us some of the best insights into how to help disadvantaged adults, whether young adults or dislocated older adults, find sustained, remunerative employment.

The sector-based, integrated approach has been found to demonstrate persistent earnings gains of 14 to 39 percent for participants after about a year of training completion, with gains persisting from three to nine years after participation in the program. This is based on a recent analysis led by Lawrence Katz and co-workers of Harvard of four randomized controlled evaluations of eight different sector-focused training programs across different workforce development providers and geographies (including Year Up, Per Scholas, Jewish Vocational Services, Wisconsin Regional Training Partnership, and Project Quest).[10] This gain is attributed not to working longer hours or to higher rates of employment but rather to holding higher-wage jobs in the target sector.

These programs have several characteristics that make them successful. They cultivate high-touch relationships with employers and involve screening, career readiness skills training, occupational skills training, job placement, wraparound support, and follow-on support. The model fills a need for training and education among individuals who would not necessarily thrive in a traditional school setting as well as dislocated workers. Training programs typically last less than six months. The programs require substantial investments per participant that range from $4,500 to $10,500. But these programs have proven to be cost-effective when compared to earnings gains by participants after three to nine years. Below we describe in more detail some of the important aspects of these programs:

Screening: An intensive screening process can last up to seven days and have varying requirements. For example, the screening identifies participants who are interested in long-term employment in the specific sector and have basic skills that are necessary for success (e.g., literacy and math, sometimes a high school diploma or GED). While often highly motivated, individuals usually lack traditional postsecondary degrees and are unemployed or underemployed prior to the program.

Career Readiness Skills Training and Services: Career readiness skills are commonly known as "soft skills" or "social skills." Organizations work with participants on topics such as time management and communication. These skills are considered as important as if not more important than occupation-specific skills in today's job market. Since technology increasingly performs the formal procedural components of numerous job tasks, judgment, collaboration, and problem-solving skills are more valuable.[11]

Occupational Skills Training: Occupational skills training is a necessary component of helping individuals successfully enter a higher-wage job in an attractive sector. Key features of the training include targeting high-wage sectors and earning an industry-recognized credential. The programs help participants develop transferable and certified skills, filling the gap where employers have mixed incentives to do it themselves.

Job Placement: Sector-based programs often have specific employers that they work with to tailor their program and ensure that the participants are prepared to meet the needs of the employer. In addition to the skills training, the programs have a job placement arm that benefits from the strong, existing relationship. The intermediation reduces the costs of onboarding newly trained employees and can help if any challenges arise in the transition period. In addition, the program is able to bridge barriers to entry that applicants face because of a lack of social capital, limited job referral networks, or employer willingness to look beyond traditional applicants.

Wraparound Support: Wraparound support refers to ways in which programs help participants navigate some of the challenges that can affect their ability to work. Such support could include assistance with transportation, child care, or unexpected emergencies.

Follow-up Support: Recognizing that the first thirty to sixty days on the job are critical, organizations provide regular and personal communication to support participants in their new job. In addition, participants receive coaching on how to think about advancement in their role.

Among these various aspects of these programs, occupational skills training that leads to an industry-recognized credential and aligns with the specific sector's employers is key. Such programs provide an important bridge to help some of the more economically insecure individuals in the labor market find and hold jobs in better-paying industries with growth opportunities.

Many of these programs, or elements of them, are delivered through a range of venues and institutions that provide adult training and education, often funded through the federal government's Workforce Innovation and Opportunity Act (WIOA) of 2014. Recent years have seen significant innovation and experimentation in the delivery of these programs across various providers. In the following sections, we highlight some of the important institutions and programs that currently constitute our approach to adult education and training, drawing heavily on the work of Task Force member Paul Osterman.[12] As we look ahead, identifying and scaling up the best of these will become more important, not less, to the country's social and economic well-being in the decades to come.

PUBLIC AND NONPROFIT TRAINING PROGRAMS

COMMUNITY COLLEGES AND INTERMEDIARIES

The linchpin of America's training ecosystem is its roughly 1,100 community colleges. As the nation's leading provider of training, community colleges enroll close to seven million students in for-credit courses annually, of whom 46 percent are over age twenty-two and 64 percent are part-time students. A majority of these older students are in vocational programs. In addition, another five million people take noncredit courses. Although noncredit courses are poorly tracked, most are vocational and populated by adults who attend part-time. Community college students in credit courses are disproportionally minority, low-income, and first-generation college students. Community colleges play multiple roles. Approximately 30 percent of students transfer to four-year schools, with the remainder of credit students receiving two-year degrees or certificates. They also help employers train incumbent workers and can be part of regional economic development strategies to attract new businesses.

As highlighted earlier, economic research has shown that degrees and certificates obtained from community colleges often lead to higher employment and earnings.[13] But to deliver on their potential, community colleges need to assist a larger share of students to complete their studies and attain degrees. Fewer than 40 percent of students who enroll in these schools complete a certificate or degree from any institution within six years. In many cases, community college students juggle coursework with adult responsibilities such as full-time employment or child care, and these competing demands surely explain (at least in part) why a substantial fraction of enrollees do not complete a degree. Programs that provide additional funding and structure to enable community college students to enroll full-time and proceed through a well-defined program of study have been shown to be highly effective in boosting degree completion rates.[14]

Many community colleges are developing innovative, new models and partnerships that integrate elements of sectoral-based training into their offerings. For example, partnerships that leverage the expertise of community colleges and the private sector are emerging to teach needed technology-oriented skills. Google has partnered with twenty-five community colleges to offer what it calls IT Support Professional Certificates.[15] Another example is IBM's P-TECH program, launched in 2011, which links high schools, local industries, and community colleges and enables students to earn both their high school diploma and a two-year associate's degree in STEM-related fields such as cybersecurity. Like many of the sectoral employment programs, P-TECH targets students from underserved backgrounds.

Community college success requires sustained engagement with local employers as well as a broader regional commitment from both the public and private sectors to invest in workforce development. One example that struck MIT researchers as particularly valuable was found in Fort Pierce, Florida, at Indian River State College. Strong leadership, regional partnerships, and a commitment to diversity, equity, and inclusion were helping the college keep up with the healthy growth trends and increasingly diverse demographics in its region while balancing the different needs of both urban and rural counties in its service area. With colleagues at the Community College Research Center at Teachers College, Columbia University, researchers identified four factors that contributed to creating an effective program at Indian River State College.[16] First, strong regional partnerships exist among economic development leaders, workforce development boards, industry, and the college. These translate into collaborations around particular training programs such as that with Florida Power & Light, which supports the electronic engineering and nuclear technology programs that train technicians and upskill engineers in a lab with equipment provided by the utility. Similarly, Disney and other media companies support students' digital media portfolio development through internships and exhibitions. The Cleveland Clinic health system has also created two certificate programs, in medical informatics and medical coding, and a longer-term program in anesthesia technology to help upskill nurses at the clinic. Second, the school developed a collaborative approach to the creation of these programs, engaging faculty, staff, and community members in assessing progress over time and looking ahead at issues like demographic and technological change. Third, the college then uses data to help improve its programs, regularly reviewing detailed data at the school and program level based on specific demographic and other characteristics (e.g., race and ethnicity, enrollment status, first time in college, first-generation college student). Finally, through active fundraising, the school has been able to invest in state-of-the-art facilities that have benefited students and the community at large through partnerships with the local community to support student learning, skills development, and employability.

Many similar examples exist in community colleges across the country. Like labor markets, they are grounded in regional economies with a unique set of institutions, industries, governing boards, state policies regarding funding, and the like. Nevertheless, recent research has shown us what makes for successful programs and provides a path forward for expanding and scaling up these programs.

One approach that appears to enhance outcomes for students enrolled in community colleges (as well as those not in school) involves so-called intermediary programs (some of which could also be categorized as sectoral training programs). These intermediaries are nonprofit organizations that craft and implement sectoral training programs, often working directly with employers to identify skills training that will prepare students for existing jobs, as well as community colleges that provide specific training. They develop programs that are characterized by close relationships with employers (the "dual customer" model), support services and counseling for clients, and substantial investments in training.[17] To achieve the close relationship with employers, intermediary staff develop expertise in industry and employer needs. Project QUEST in San Antonio, for instance, works with local firms to identify future job openings and then recruits low-wage workers to train them for those positions. Participants engage in remedial education and attend weekly group meetings that encourage motivation and support life skills development. They receive financial assistance to cover transportation and other needs. A rigorous evaluation of the QUEST program[18] (part of the evaluation discussed earlier in this section) found that participants earned significantly more than equivalent control group members who were not randomly selected into the program. By year nine, the gap exceeded $5,000 per year in additional earnings for graduates of the program. Another similar program, Jewish Vocational Services (JVS) in Boston, helps employers construct career ladders within the company, as well as fill their hiring needs. JVS has long-term relationships with local firms, such as hospitals, where it trains workers in low-wage positions such as food service to move into better-paying, patient-facing jobs.

SCHOOL-BASED VOCATIONAL TRAINING AND APPRENTICESHIPS

Another area of innovation in recent years involves high schools and immediate postsecondary education institutions that can play an important role in providing immediately marketable job skills.[19] High school CTE may be integrated into comprehensive high schools or in dedicated vocational high school facilities. New models for CTE programs have proliferated in recent years.[20]

Their core characteristic is to better integrate work experience with the traditional classroom. Examples include the Pathways to Prosperity Network and the IBM P-TECH schools (mentioned earlier). Another strategy is to work with existing schools and update the traditional apprenticeship model by linking high school classes with work experience. Workers benefit from apprenticeships by receiving a skills-based education that prepares them for well-paying jobs, while employers benefit by recruiting and retaining a skilled workforce.[21] Examples include CareerWise Colorado, the Georgia Youth Apprenticeship Program, and the Toyota FAME model.

These models draw their inspiration from European vocational education and training (VET) programs, which build on the strong relationships between government and "social partners"—employer associations and unions. As Task Force member Kathleen Thelen and co-author Christian Ibsen found in their analysis of German and Danish VET programs, these programs support national objectives around developing a skilled workforce for the private sector and increasing inclusion of those who may have weak ties to the labor market, though the German and Danish cases underscore the trade-offs that exist in achieving these two goals.[22] The justified criticism of such programs is that they sort students during their postsecondary schooling (often along class lines) into either a vocational or an academic track, with little permeability between the two. VET programs focus on middle-skilled occupations (e.g., electrician, nurse, technician) and provide two to four years of training that includes workplace learning and more theoretical instruction in the classroom. The systems have four distinctive features: (1) VET occurs through firm-sponsored training (with associated classroom-based training); (2) the programs rely heavily on the private sector to take on apprentices and pay for their training; (3) firms must train broadly, not narrowly, in skills and competencies defined by committees comprising representatives from industry, government, and labor; and (4) nationally defined standards help ensure consistent content and quality. Firms are encouraged to participate in such programs by "beneficial constraints" that create incentives for firms to take a longer view on investments in training and in workers more broadly. These constraints are embedded in the "institutional ecosystem" in these countries, including industrial relations institutions (sectoral or national-level collective bargaining with unions), strong employment protections, and institutions that support worker participation within firms.

While such programs are country-specific and do not readily translate to the highly decentralized and individualistic (as opposed to collectivist) US context, they are worth studying as apprenticeship programs expand in the US. Indeed, the VET model has inspired significant investments in recent years in apprenticeship programs in the US. Funding at the federal and state levels led to a 50 percent increase in the number of apprenticeships in 2019, to more than 600,000.[23] While still a miniscule number compared to programs in Europe, innovation and experimentation with apprenticeships are leading to successful models and best practices that are also expanding beyond the traditional apprenticeship fields of the trades and manufacturing.

One model in the US that has received high marks in recent years is found in South Carolina. Through a focus on strengthening its workforce training strategy, the state now has what is considered one of the nation's most successful apprenticeship programs at the technical college level, and now with a youth apprenticeship in Charleston starting in high school. Founded in 2007, the state's program, Apprenticeship Carolina, has grown to more than 30,000 registered apprenticeships across every county and enjoys the participation of all sixteen of the state's two-year technical colleges. This initiative allows the state to help employers fill out US Department of Labor apprenticeship credentialing paperwork free of charge, and to formalize a variety of local programs. The program has been embraced by both small and large companies, including South Carolina's numerous Germany-based firms.

In Charleston, the high school apprenticeship program was initiated in 2014 by six smaller employers seeking skilled workers. It consists of a collaboration among employers, the area's technical college, and the Chamber of Commerce. The state provides a $1,000 tax credit to participating companies, and the Chamber of Commerce and a state program pays the technical college tuition. Employers cover the wages of student apprentices, who work part-time and during the summer while taking math and science courses at their own high school and coursework at the technical college. Firms choose their own apprenticeship hires, who range from sixteen to eighteen years of age, and students earn about a year's worth of credit toward a two-year associate's degree. Participating employers have spent $5 million since the beginning of the program, with most of the cost borne by small employers—although the city's largest employers, including Boeing and Bosch, have since joined. As of 2018, the program had ninety-four students enrolled, and 232 former apprentices had been hired by hosting firms.[24]

Another example of public-private partnership in training at the city level comes from Detroit. In recent years, Detroit has been adding automotive jobs, but not assembly jobs for factory workers, rather jobs in engineering and design work. That changed in February 2019 when Fiat Chrysler Automobiles (FCA) announced a deal with the state and city to convert an old engine plant and update an old assembly plant to produce new Jeeps.[25] FCA enlisted the city's workforce agency, Detroit at Work, to recruit five thousand workers and committed that United Auto Workers (UAW) members and Detroit residents would be considered first for jobs. As of October 2020, more than 16,000 Detroiters had been screened, more than 10,000 had completed an application, and more than 5,000 had been invited for interviews. FCA has extended 4,100 job offers to Detroit residents.

The state and city offered FCA large incentive packages, including acquiring 200 acres of property near the old plants for the plant renewal and expansion. FCA also received a commitment for property tax abatement. This recruitment deal was controversial and is still viewed with some skepticism. It is an important test case for Detroit at Work, which is responsible for preparing Detroit residents for the new assembly jobs and establishing the city as a go-to source for manufacturing talent. To those leading the effort, the partnership among FCA, the city, and Detroit at Work demonstrates that Detroit's talent recruitment model can succeed.

Job seekers in Detroit have access to a wide range of support services, including document review, hands-on training in common manufacturing practices, math tutoring, interview practice, and transportation assistance. The Employment Service/One-Stops played a key role through-out this process. This deal also requires that FCA provide information that would enable an effective recruitment and pre-screening effort. FCA and Detroit at Work spent a year learning about each other's systems in order to identify and prepare a workforce that would succeed at FCA. A number of other commitments by FCA regarding further upskilling at the com-pany and across the city further expanded the scope of the partnership.

Most of the new jobs at FCA are assembly line positions starting at around $17 an hour. This work is often repetitive and physically chal-lenging. But these jobs lead to union- and employer-provided benefits. The very large number of applications submitted makes clear that these positions are attractive.

DISLOCATED WORKERS

The examples provided above across community colleges, intermediaries, and vocational training providers represent successful models for creat-ing pathways forward for the majority of adults who are not on a path toward a four-year degree. Many of these experimentally verified training programs are effective in moving low-wage workers and young adults up the job ladder. But the understanding of what is effective for middle-aged employees who are dislocated by trade, technological change, or even COVID-19 is considerably weaker. Most experience with retraining middle-aged and older employees comes from programs funded through WIOA and from training funded by a separate program that targets workers who lose their jobs as a result of trade (the Trade Adjustment Assistance program, or TAA). Evaluations of these programs show mixed results: a TAA study suggested that close to 75 percent of participants found jobs, but with earnings replacement ratios of 75 to 85 percent, depending on age. Other well-designed and well-managed programs with community colleges (as part of the TAA Community College and Career Training program) reported significant positive employment gains.[26] Much work remains to understand how best to serve dislocated workers, particularly those with less education. Significant barriers exist for these workers, including how they perceive training and the challenges they face in obtaining it.[27] No doubt the COVID-19 crisis will create ample opportunity to try to help such workers, and the country should accordingly invest in developing and rigorously evaluating programs that offer promising approaches.

PRIVATE SECTOR INVESTMENT IN TRAINING

Insofar as one of the key success factors for training programs is close engagement with the private sector, it is reasonable to ask what role the private sector plays in training the country's workforce. As it turns out, this is a challenging question to answer because of the paucity of data on firm-based training. Most of our current understanding is based on anecdotes and surveys that are at least ten to fifteen years old. We know that employers hesitate to make large, up-front investments in their workers' general portable skills since workers may take those skills to another employer to earn a higher wage. Still, before the COVID-19 pandemic, when many companies saw tight labor markets into the foreseeable future, there were numerous examples of large firms investing in internal training programs to provide upskilling opportunities for their workers. IBM, for example, has installed a company-wide facility that uses AI to recommend personalized learning content to employees, who are expected to spend a minimum of forty hours in training and professional development each year. Training is offered to all employees at every level of the firm, and in 2019, the median trainee spent fifty-two hours in training.[28] In another example, in 2019 Amazon committed $700 million to provide 100,000 employees, roughly a third of Amazon's US workforce at the time, with access to training programs through 2025. This includes their Career Choice program for warehouse workers, which provides on-site education and training in growth sectors (IT, health care) outside Amazon for employees who have been with the company for at least a year.

These anecdotes, however, don't give us a full picture about firm-based training. Filling this gap, a recent national survey by Paul Osterman of what training employers provide and what training workers undertake on their own,[29] provides some insights into how adults obtain their skills and the role of the private sector. In a representative survey of roughly 3,700 working adults between the ages of twenty-four and sixty-four,

approximately half of the adults surveyed said they had received training from their employers in the past year, while about 20 percent had
taken part in some form of training on their own, a relatively high share
of which (about three quarters) was online. Workers at the lower end
of the wage and skill distribution received less training. The survey also
found substantial racial and ethnic disparities in access to employer-
provided training. These disparities remained even after controlling for
a full range of personal characteristics, employer characteristics, and job
skills requirements.[30] While it is hard to say whether or not it is a problem that nearly half the working population had not received any training in the previous year, it is certainly problematic that substantial racial
and ethnic disparities exist regarding employer investments in training.
These findings point to the important role public policy, publicly funded
training programs, and nonprofits can play in equalizing opportunities
to improve skills.

KEY AREAS MOVING FORWARD: FUNDING, REGIONAL COMPACTS, AND INNOVATION

While the US lacks the firm social contract that elsewhere drives cooperation between different stakeholders in the skills training system, it can
build a stronger foundation for delivering quality training at scale. Here
we highlight three dimensions that are important to moving forward:
funding, regional commitments, and innovation.

FUNDING

Educational and training programs have faced declining support across
the board, precisely the opposite of what is needed at this critical juncture
for workers. For example, government funding accounts for just under
65 percent of community college revenue. Between 2000 and 2019, total
funding per full-time student from state, local, and federal sources for
community colleges was flat in real (inflation-adjusted) terms, while
demands on, and expectations of, the system increased considerably.
Federal funding for adult job training, adult basic education, and high
school CTE have all declined. The Workforce Investment Act/Workforce

Innovation and Opportunity Act spending between fiscal years 2001 and 2019 fell from $4.62 billion to $2.82 billion (see figure 4.1). This decline is substantial, but even it overestimates the limited funds for training. Because WIOA funds are used along with Wagner-Peyser Act funding to support the job centers, estimates are that less than 30 percent of WIOA funding is expended on training. The lack of resources for training is particularly troubling because the successful intermediaries described above require nontrivial investments.

REGIONAL COMMITMENT

A focus on a regional commitment to education and training makes sense because labor markets are regional and because public labor market programs, adult education, community colleges, and school systems

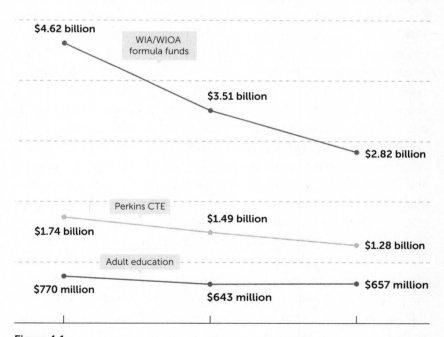

Figure 4.1
Workforce Investment Act/Workforce Innovation and Opportunity Act (WIA/WIOA) Spending, Fiscal Years 2001–2019. *Source:* National Skills Coalition, https://www.nationalskillscoalition.org/news/blog/budget-analysis-2021-request-has-important-skills-proposals-but-big-cuts-to-labor-and-safety-net-programs.

are all best managed by state or regional leaders, who can coordinate at the state or regional level (including across state boundaries, as in the Greater Washington, DC, area).[31] That said, there is a deeper requirement than good management: a shared commitment by employers, community groups and unions, and government and education leaders to build and support a system. Several states exemplify this kind of commitment. For example, Massachusetts, North Carolina, and Tennessee are widely admired for their creative workforce development systems. But even in these best-practice states, limited resources constrain scale.[32]

The City of Boston provides an example of concerted regional commitment over decades. In the late 1970s, state government and the high-tech business community came together to form the Bay State Skills Corporation, which provided public and private dollars for job training. In 1982 the Boston business community more broadly supported the Boston Compact, an early example of current "promise programs" that provided financial support for postsecondary education to all Boston high school graduates. In 1996, Bay State Skills and another state economic development agency were merged to form the Commonwealth Corporation (CommCorp), which is funded by a state appropriation and which manages, among other training programs, an incumbent worker training initiative financed by a portion of the state unemployment insurance tax. The state investments support a wide range of training efforts and cooperate with two large union programs, Local 1199's health training and the Hotel and Restaurant Employees Union BEST job training program. Another important player is the Boston Private Industry Council (PIC), the oversight agency for WIOA funding. The Boston PIC membership includes high-level corporate leadership and is effective in helping to link training programs with jobs. Additionally, two of the most innovative intermediaries in the country, JVS and Year Up, are based in Boston. In 2018, Massachusetts created a coordinated, statewide umbrella that unites the state's sixteen regional workforce boards and twenty-five to thirty local workforce centers into a single coalition called MassHire. Announced in the fall of 2020, MassHire will provide a template for a new state-based training and career pathway model in manufacturing sponsored by the US Department of Defense (MassBridge).

INNOVATION

Where research has identified specific programs and practices that work, the challenge ahead is scaling up and replicating these successes. Meeting this challenge requires investment, institutional reforms, and a regional commitment by the full range of public and private actors. Alongside these successful examples, there is much room for innovation. Here we summarize several promising directions.

Skills Standards Modeled on those in Germany, skills standards were introduced into the US policy discussion during the Clinton administration. The rationale is that standardization of credentials would enable people to be more mobile across employers and even geographies, while at the same time providing assurance to employers about the qualifications of a new hire. While the idea is attractive in the abstract, important questions remain. The deepest problem is that employers do not seem to pay attention to credentials except in tightly defined circumstances (e.g., some IT certifications), a limitation that has been demonstrated in two large-scale surveys.[33] For reasons that are not fully understood, employers simply do not seem to find the credentials relevant. For skills standards to succeed, training institutions and employers will need to collaborate to define standards that are job-relevant and credibly certified.

Labor Market Information Transparency Many efforts by both public and private sector actors seek to better collect and promulgate information on the state of local labor markets: occupational openings, compensation, skills requirements, payoffs for obtaining different credentials, and the track record of different training providers in providing these credentials. Markets do not readily disclose such information, leading to endemic information shortfalls that, if redressed, could lead to better decision-making by workers, employers, and training providers. New experiments are also under way with developing digital records of individuals' skills and competencies that could help them navigate the labor market over time.[34] While it is hard to argue against improved information, information per se is not a substitute for investments in worker skills or in the quality of skills providers. Moreover, simply providing public data on the quality of skills providers may be insufficient to weed out weak providers.

Individual Training Accounts Adequate funding is a major problem for all components of the public job training and readjustment system. Individual Training Accounts (ITAs) aim to address these challenges by providing opportunities for adults to save for education and training using pretax dollars that would be matched by public contributions.[35] One issue here is how to structure the accounts so that low-paid workers, who may very well find funding contributions challenging, can benefit. The deeper issue is the same as that which we have already identified: absent careful quality certification and rigorous oversight, history suggests that low-quality providers will proliferate and absorb training dollars.[36] ITAs are an idea worth exploring, but they must be structured to ensure that ITA providers meet quality standards and that low-paid workers have sufficient funds to access training (possibly through subsidies).

NEW PEDAGOGIES: ONLINE EDUCATION

With the vast potential for innovation in online learning—something that was essentially infeasible two decades ago—new ideas for pedagogy are proliferating. Examples are certificate programs such as those provided by Oracle and Microsoft, boot camps, online courses, blended online and in-person offerings, machine-supervised learning, and augmented and virtual reality learning environments. A full accounting of the number and scope of these new models is lacking, although efforts to classify and track them, such as that undertaken by Credential Engine, a nonprofit founded in 2016, are under way.

Some of these innovations hold great promise for improving pedagogy, lowering costs, and facilitating scaling up. As an example, online classes enable community college students to more easily combine working with education and training. Indeed, the proportion of students studying fully online who are enrolled within fifty miles of their homes is increasing.[37]

While it remains in early development, online education has evolved rapidly with the spread of broadband technology. Since they were first introduced by colleges and universities in 2012, massive open online courses, or MOOCs, have grown and have enrolled 100 million people on a global basis.[38] Hybrids of online education are now emerging as well, in which students combine online work with in-person courses at an educational institution.

Task Force member and MIT's Vice President for Open Learning Sanjay Sarma and Research Advisory Board member William Bonvillian studied the growth of the digital learning sector. They focused on tools that can be quickly scaled up and delivered, often at lower cost than traditional programs. Much of workforce education must be "hands-on," so online elements work best when blended with in-person guidance and work on equipment.[39] The COVID-19 crisis accelerated the development of this field as millions of students and teachers shifted to remote learning for health and safety reasons. In this scramble to move online amid the pandemic, many working adults had to attend training sessions, conferences, and events through videoconferencing, further deepening the penetration of online modalities.

Insofar as most of the tools for online education are less than a decade old, it is unsurprising that online education faces many challenges on its way to achieving its full potential. The completion rate for individual, stand-alone online courses is quite low, though that may not be a meaningful metric since a large share of online enrollment is likely low-cost window shopping.

Of course, online education need not merely replicate traditional offerings. One innovative model offers groups of related courses with certificates that attest to work-related skills that can translate into job opportunities. As the workforce increasingly engages in lifelong learning, online skills provision is increasingly useful for upgrading skills and adding complementary know-how on top of an established background. YouTube, for example, offers an ever-expanding cornucopia of widely used "how-to" videos. Online learning will likely be even more important for workforce education than for traditional educational venues, though the move to online schooling during the COVID-19 pandemic may tip that balance.

One result of the coronavirus-driven rush to online learning tools has been an acceleration in the study of what works best in this medium. Cognitive psychology and education studies provide extensive guidance on how to bring learning science into online education. One commonsense lesson is that video lectures that lack interactive content have limited learning value because students find it challenging to pay attention. A better approach is to intersperse lectures with participatory discussions and to restructure presentations into a series of "bite-size chunks," each lasting about ten minutes or less. This is easier with prerecorded, asynchronous videos than with Zoom lectures.

A second lesson is that creating "desirable difficulties," where the learner has to struggle a bit with the material, enhances learning. Additional effective techniques include spreading out lessons, so that learning occurs and is reiterated over a period of weeks and months; and providing frequent low-stakes assessments and feedback, which increases engagement. These practices can be readily built into online programs.

A revolution in educational content and delivery may well change how schooling and training are executed. A great deal of ongoing experimentation, a smattering of successes and failures, and much unrealized potential remain, as does a clear need for evaluation to determine what is effective. Future workforce education will build on the capabilities of emerging technologies, including AI-powered tutoring systems, virtual and augmented reality, "gamified" and simulated learning environments, and collaborative tools. These tools will become increasingly central to skills training provision, may be virtuously combined with new delivery modalities that expand access, and offer the potential for broader access, lower-cost delivery, and greater learner engagement at a time of growing need for workforce upskilling and lifelong learning.

5

JOB QUALITY

As documented in chapter 2, the US has not translated rising productivity into commensurate improvements in job opportunities and earnings for the majority of workers during the last four decades. The poor quality of jobs open to US workers lacking four-year college degrees or specialized credentials provides one of the starkest examples of this failure. Low-wage US workers earn substantially less than low-wage workers in almost all other wealthy industrialized countries. For example, the OECD estimates that they earn approximately 25 percent less than their Canadian counterparts.[1] This substantial earnings difference is particularly striking in light of the many commonalities between the US and Canada, including legal and institutional environments, education systems, industrial structures, and deep trade integration. Notably, Canadians workers have access to universal, publicly provided health care.

The divergence between the upward path of productivity growth and the near plateauing of median wage growth among US workers is not an inevitable consequence of technology, globalization, or market forces. Rather, a set of US-specific institutional and policy choices failed to blunt—and in some cases magnified—the consequences of technological and globalization pressures on the US labor market. To contend effectively with these challenges requires institutional and policy reforms that realign labor market opportunities with the rising productivity and societal wealth that the US has reaped from decades of innovation and investments in human and physical capital. These reforms include crafting and enforcing fair labor standards, setting well-calibrated federal minimum wage policies, extending the scope and flexibility of the unemployment insurance system, and transforming the US employer-based health insurance provision into a system with portable benefits.

The US also needs to reevaluate its devotion to pure shareholder capitalism—which has arguably helped fuel the drive to curtail wages and benefits for low-wage workers. While shareholder capitalism can plausibly be credited with some of the productive dynamism of the US economy, it needs to be balanced with greater emphasis on creating a system that bolsters the skills and compensation of all workers.

Fixing the job quality problem won't be easy. The breakdown in upward mobility and diminished protections for workers occurred gradually over many years and won't be fixed overnight. But some necessary steps are clear. Here we address policy changes needed in three important areas that could have long-term impact on job quality in the country: (1) reforming unemployment insurance, (2) establishing meaningful minimum wage regulations, and (3) restoring workers as stakeholders in collective bargaining and corporate decision-making. Other steps are needed of course, including finding a way to provide health coverage to workers independent of their employment status, though this is a topic we don't address in depth in this book. Relatedly, some have advocated for a universal basic income (UBI) to provide low-income people greater economic security. While initial evidence in developed countries suggests that a guaranteed income can improve people's general economic well-being,[2] our focus in this book is on policies that make *work* better. UBI will generally not fulfill that purpose in industrialized countries, though it has other benefits (and costs) that merit close study.

UNEMPLOYMENT INSURANCE: HOW DID WE GET WHERE WE ARE TODAY?

Unemployment insurance (UI) is America's first line of defense against the financial toll of job loss for workers who become involuntarily unemployed. The COVID-19 crisis has spotlighted the weaknesses of the UI system, which was established by the Social Security Act of 1935 and operates as a complex partnership between state and federal authorities.

The program was originally intended to offer only modest benefits over a limited period of time. But as funds accumulated from the payroll taxes set aside to fund the system, there was a move in the 1950s to set benefits across the US that were consistent and more generous— approximately half of a worker's prior wage (up to a set maximum) for at least twenty-six weeks. That structure largely held for several decades. But starting in the early 1980s, the wage replacement rates began falling as antitax sentiments grew and public finances deteriorated in many states.

The University of Maryland's Professor Katharine Abraham, working with Task Force Advisory Board member Susan Houseman and Christopher O'Leary, of the W. E. Upjohn Institute for Employment Research, took a close look at the system.[3] Their work highlights overdue modifications needed in the rules determining who is covered by the system and what it takes to qualify for benefits among those who are nominally covered. The US UI system excludes the self-employed, for instance. That category traditionally encompasses people who own their own businesses and employ others. However, increasingly it includes many relatively low-paid service workers, including maids, babysitters, and gig workers whose work is mediated by online platforms or mobile apps. "Changes in technology and other factors are likely to contribute to growing rates of self-employment in the coming years, and many of these workers are likely to be exposed to considerable income fluctuation risk," write the researchers.

The reality is that companies have some discretion in how they classify their workers. As noted by Abraham, Houseman, and O'Leary, there's little chance that a classification decision will be challenged by regulators, and some worry that many firms err on the side of labeling workers as independent contractors in order to avoid having them qualify for jobless benefits. One example is large farms, which often label their workers contractors.

Workers lost a major battle in this fight in the 2020 election, when California voters backed a ballot proposal funded by DoorDash, Uber, and Lyft that dictated that their drivers continue to be classified as independent contractors. It was the most expensive ballot contest in state history, and its impact was almost immediately felt in a range of industries. Major supermarkets, for instance, swiftly announced they would lay off their delivery drivers and replace them with app-based delivery services.

Even when employed in UI-covered jobs, low-wage and part-time workers may have trouble qualifying for benefits. As of the beginning of 2019, workers in five states—Arizona, Indiana, Michigan, Ohio, and South Carolina—who work twenty hours a week at the state's minimum wage for six months wouldn't accumulate enough earnings to qualify. In twenty-three other states, working twenty hours a week for three months at the state's minimum wage wouldn't be enough, even if the workers met other eligibility requirements.

These rules mean that the UI system fails to insure some of the lowest-paid workers in the most precarious jobs, even though these workers are employed in traditional direct-hire jobs that in theory are covered. The growth of scheduling algorithms in retail, hospitality, and other service industries contributes to the problem as workers in these industries face fluctuating hours and schedules that can make it especially hard to accrue the earnings history they need to qualify for benefits.

Within this restrictive system, some states have implemented policies that have the effect of further limiting enrollment. Florida, for example, moved to an online system in 2011 that was available only in English and required applicants to complete a forty-five-question online skills assessment. Some of these requirements were later changed after legal challenges, but the filing process remains difficult.

One indicator that the UI system has failed to keep pace with the changing structure of jobs is the declining share of the unemployed who receive benefits. That share has generally trended downward over the last four decades, rising only when the economy strengthens sufficiently to bring workers into full-time, direct-hire employment. Since 2011, the share of unemployed receiving UI benefits has remained below 30 percent. The percentage of unemployed workers who received regular state unemployment benefits had previously fluctuated over time, but only once before, in the mid-1980s, did it drop below that level. The rate rose to 40 percent during the 2008–2009 recession but then plunged and hasn't recovered.

This decline was driven by particularly sharp cutbacks in a handful of states: In just eight states, most in the Southeast, the share of unemployed workers receiving jobless benefits has fallen to between 10 percent and 15 percent. At the other end of the spectrum are eight, mostly northeastern states, where the rate at which unemployed workers receive benefits remains above 40 percent—including Massachusetts and New Jersey, which have rates well over 50 percent. "Instead of viewing unemployment insurance as a program to support productive job search and improve the efficiency of job matches, the policy posture in some states is that unemployment insurance is simply a business cost to be minimized," Abraham and co-authors note.

One reason for this decline can be traced to the recession of 2008–2009, when soaring joblessness led many states to deplete their trust funds—the money set aside in good times to help states get through recessions. Rather than seek to rebuild those trust funds during the recent recovery, some states responded by reducing the generosity of benefits or the maximum duration they could be received.

The declining fraction of workers who are successful in accessing the system is in part a reflection of changes in the economy. Researchers have found a positive correlation between the rate at which workers receive unemployment insurance and the rate of unionization.[4] "One possible reason is that unions may provide valuable information about the UI application process to members who are laid off. Declining rates of unionization may well have contributed to the decline in the recipiency rate," Abraham and her colleagues note. Other factors often cited are the growth of "nonstandard" work arrangements and the polarization of the job market, which expands the share of precarious jobs where workers may not qualify for UI benefits.

These facts point to the compelling need to modernize and reinforce this crucial piece of the social safety net for workers. As the current COVID-19 crisis underscores, the causes of involuntary job loss are numerous, with technological displacement being only one of them. To its credit, the federal government enabled expanded jobless benefits in the spring of 2020 as part of its stimulus efforts in response to the COVID-19 crisis.

Abraham and colleagues propose four sensible modifications to the unemployment insurance system to make the program more accessible and equitable: (1) allowing workers to count their most recent earnings toward eligibility determination, (2) establishing UI eligibility based on hours rather than earnings (which currently makes it harder for low-wage workers to obtain UI), (3) dropping the requirement that the unemployed seek full-time work, and (4) reforming partial unemployment insurance benefits to better protect workers who lose a substantial fraction of their work hours or earnings without losing their jobs.

Alongside modernizing the unemployment insurance system, the US must carefully consider how independent contractors are classified to assure that they are truly independent. The US effectively applies two distinct sets of laws and regulations to employment: one guarantees UI, workers' compensation, and some mandatory benefits to traditional full-time direct-hire employees; the other provides few protections to "independent" worker categories, including contractors, domestic workers, gig workers, and, in many cases, part-time workers. The distinction between these two employment categories has arguably grown more ambiguous over time, while the incentive for employers to reclassify employees as independent workers has only increased. There is no ready solution to this problem, but it is clear that employment policy and regulation requires innovation to keep pace with the changing structure of work.

ESTABLISHING MEANINGFUL MINIMUM WAGE REGULATIONS

A key lever affecting the quality of jobs available to low-paid workers is the level of the minimum wage, which is the lowest hourly wage that can legally be paid to most US workers.[5] During times of tight labor markets, as in the expansion just before the COVID-19 pandemic, employers were forced to bump up salaries, even when they weren't required to do so by state or federal law, just to acquire and hold the workers they needed. Employers often complained that their low-wage workers would jump to different employers for small wage differences, creating costly turnover as they were forced to constantly hire and train new workers. In reality, it is a healthy manifestation of competition when employers in a tight labor market raise pay to attract and retain workers.

Until recently there was little pressure to raise wages from state or federal authorities. Keeping a low minimum wage has been viewed by many state officials as key to luring employers to open new operations in their jurisdictions. Meanwhile, periodic increases in the federal minimum wage to counteract the effect of inflation have been regularly stymied by strong ideological and business opposition. While many free market conservatives believe there is no role for a minimum wage in a competitive market, businesses are more inclined to argue that the federal government should not be setting a national minimum wage. Rather, they argue that this role is best left to states since a suitable minimum wage in a poorer and lower-cost-of-living state like Mississippi, for instance, might be well below that in wealthy Massachusetts or New York. There is merit to this argument: federal minimum wage regulation should set a national wage floor that states and localities can build on—as occurs regularly.

Between 1979 and 2016, there were 138 prominent state minimum wage changes.[6] Logically, states with high wage levels and high costs of living, such as New York, Massachusetts, Washington, and California, tend to set higher minimum wage levels than other states. Seattle, for example, was the first US city to mandate a $15 per hour minimum wage in 2014. The move sparked widespread consternation among businesses, which argued it would encourage companies to move outside city limits to avoid the cost. The higher wage was phased in over time—allowing smaller businesses several years to reach the $15 minimum—and 2021 is the first year all employers will be covered by the mandate. Meanwhile, Florida voters approved raising that state's minimum wage to $15 per hour in a series of steps over six years. Over 60 percent of voters approved the necessary amendment to Florida's constitution.

Prior to the 1990s, most states did not set their own minimum wages but instead left this responsibility to the federal minimum wage. The reason that states have stepped in to raise minimum wages over the last three decades is easy to discern from figure 5.1: the real value of the federal minimum wage has fallen nearly continuously—with only brief course corrections—since 1980. In those decades, ideological opposition and business lobbying have kept the minimum wage's nominal value largely fixed while inflation has inexorably eroded its real value. In 2020, the real value of the US federal minimum was essentially equal to its real value

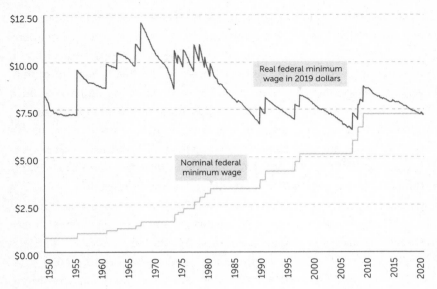

Figure 5.1
US Federal Minimum Hourly Wage, 1979–2020. *Source:* US Bureau of Labor Statistics and Federal Reserve Bank of St Louis (fred.stlouis.org). The real minimum wage was calculated using the Consumer Price Index, Urban Consumers: All Items in US City Average, December 2019 = 100.

in 1950—seven decades earlier—and approximately 35 percent below its real value in 1979.

The best available evidence indicates that well-calibrated minimum wages exert modest to undetectable adverse effects on employment while reducing household poverty. They are particularly effective at bolstering the earnings of minority workers, who are overrepresented at the lower tail of the US wage distribution. The erosion of the US federal minimum wage, itself a deliberate policy decision, has magnified US earnings inequality, retarded the earnings growth of low-paid US workers, and likely further weakened the hand of labor unions in negotiating on behalf of their members. While states have an important role in calibrating minimum wages upward from the federal minimum to match their specific circumstances, the federal government aids low-wage workers and clears political roadblocks by setting a floor that every state must abide by.

There is room for minimum wage increases that do not disrupt employment and instead create positive regional ripple effects that can enhance wages for low-paid workers. Restoring the real value of the federal minimum wage to a reasonable percentage of the current national median wage would benefit workers substantially at little net economic cost.[7] Indexing this value to the median wage to counteract the erosive effect of inflation would further compound the benefits. First, it would halt the cycle of gradually eroding real minimum wage levels, which is harmful to low-wage workers. Second, relative to a status quo in which minimum wage levels tend to jump discontinuously, often in response to popular ballot initiatives, an indexed minimum wage would reduce businesses' uncertainty about the wage constraints they are likely to face going forward. As noted above, localities should retain the ability to set higher statutes, as they do currently.

The fact that well-chosen minimum wage regulations boost worker earnings while having minimal adverse effects on hiring does not imply that these policies are a "free lunch." Rather, well-calibrated minimum wage regulations function as a way to redistribute income—on a pretax basis—out of the pocket of employers and consumers and into the paychecks of low-paid workers. Research confirms that minimum wage hikes tend to reduce firms' profitability and, by raising their costs of doing business, spur them to raise prices. These higher costs can have meaningful consequences. In Germany, a substantial national minimum wage hike in 2015 caused inefficient firms to shrink while enabling more efficient firms to grow at their expense. This policy change was beneficial to workers, who received a pay increase, and to larger firms, which gained market share, but it squeezed out the smaller firms that were insufficiently productive to cover higher labor costs. This, as well as the presumably higher costs of goods that are passed on to consumers, serves as a reminder that policy choices necessarily require trade-offs.[8]

Alongside the minimum wage, numerous factors affect the quality of jobs available to workers on the lower rungs of the job market. These include the availability of sick pay, family medical leave, and maternity pay, none of which is required to be paid by US employers.[9] They also include the expectation of a stable number of weekly paid hours, stable schedule, or advance notice of work schedules, which are again nonmandatory and often not provided. Further critical job attributes include safe working conditions, financial compensation in the case of on-the-job injury or death, and access to health insurance, something which, unique among wealthy industrialized countries, the US primarily provides through employers, and generally not to low-wage workers. In almost all these respects, the US ranks poorly among wealthy industrialized countries in providing stable, secure employment to workers occupying the lower rungs of the labor market.[10]

A leading example of the precarious conditions facing low-paid US workers is found in the US health care system. While health care as a whole is viewed as a sector with good opportunities for those with limited education or training, the picture is far darker for those who don't work directly for health care systems. US Bureau of Labor Statistics (BLS) data find that in 2019, the median pay of health and personal care aides was $25,280 ($12.15 per hour), while those of certified nursing assistants was only slightly better at $29,640 ($14.25 per hour): $20,025. "Home care aides are seen as unskilled companions, or glorified babysitters, with little education and little potential," notes Paul Osterman, who adds that these workers are disproportionately female and immigrants or racial minorities.[11] While these might appear to be isolated examples, these two occupations alone accounted for more than five million US workers in 2019—that is, approximately one in twenty-five jobs—and are projected to add another 1.25 million workers over the subsequent decade.[12]

Health and personal care workers and certified nursing assistants are constrained by state "scope of practice" rules that prevent them from administering medications or assisting with many routine medical procedures. With changes to scope of practice rules, these workers could be authorized and trained to perform services such as observation of health conditions and wound treatment. This would open the way for these jobs to earn more and gain the status that would come from being viewed as integral to the larger delivery of health care to the elderly and disabled, a group whose numbers are expected to double over the next twenty-five years. Yet some employers and analysts interviewed by Osterman dismiss this possibility, since they view the motivation and ability of these workers to learn these new skills as too limited. Perhaps more important, certified nurses resist allowing lesser trained health care providers to perform many of the tasks they perform for fear of impinging on their wage and salary levels.

WORKERS AS STAKEHOLDERS

Americans' greater anxiety about the adverse impact of automation relative to that of their counterparts in other advanced nations is arguably one of the social costs of the US shareholder primacy model.[13] Workers rightly perceive that they are not guaranteed to share in the fruits of new advancements. The US is unique among market economies in venerating pure shareholder capitalism—the notion that the sole purpose of firms is to maximize shareholder value. Shareholder capitalism dictates that employees should be valued like all other intangible assets—that is, compensated at market prices and scrapped if their value to the firm falls below their cost to the firm. Within this paradigm, the personal, social, and public costs of layoffs and plant closings should not play a critical role in decision-making. While shareholder capitalism can plausibly be credited with some of the productive dynamism of the US economy, pure shareholder capitalism is due for reevaluation.

Increasingly, US businesses are engaging in that reevaluation. In August 2019, the Business Roundtable—a group made up of the CEOs of many of the US's largest corporations—issued a new "Statement on the Purpose of a Corporation," signed by 181 CEOs, committing to lead their companies for the benefit of all stakeholders—customers, employees, suppliers, communities, and shareholders. It's the first time since 1997 that the organization's principles did not state that corporations exist principally to serve shareholders. Jamie Dimon, chairman and CEO of JPMorgan Chase & Co. and chairman of the group, said at the time: "The American Dream is alive, but fraying."[14]

Bold statements are easy to make. It remains to be seen whether they are followed by meaningful change in boardrooms. There are prominent examples of large companies raising base pay levels above statutory minimum wage levels, such as Walmart and Amazon. When these firms raise their starting wages, competing firms operating in the same labor markets also improve their wage and benefit offers.[15] However, we should be skeptical that firms will raise pay simply because they recognize "workers as stakeholders." This is a costly action, and if higher pay is not matched by higher productivity, it's unclear whether managers can justify these steps to their boards or shareholders.[16] In general, creating better jobs for workers requires firms to pay higher wages and use labor more effectively. Absent the latter, firms may find that providing higher pay is unprofitable or even infeasible. As two of America's largest employers of low-paid labor, both Amazon and Walmart had come under considerable public criticism for their employment practices prior to raising their base pay. Public pressure strengthens the business case for higher pay (i.e., to avert negative publicity), but it's unlikely to work for the vast majority of firms that are less visible and less profitable than Amazon and Walmart. There is clearly a role for policy in creating incentives that make these steps attractive (or unavoidable) for employers.[17]

Labor unions that negotiate directly with employers over pay and working conditions provide a traditional alternative to either legislatively enacted regulations or public pressure campaigns. Union representation is another case in which US workers have fared more poorly compared to those in other many other advanced industrial countries. While union coverage has declined in many countries, the US rate of coverage is well below other OECD countries, as shown in figure 5.2. In the past, labor unions played a key role in counterbalancing management by representing worker interests. Indeed, there was a time in the post–World War II era when unions were arguably too strong, limiting flexibility, raising costs, and blunting incentives for technological improvements.[18]

The negotiating power of unions has declined along with their membership. Simultaneously, support for unions among the general public has actually grown in recent years, with a sharp upswing after the recession of 2008–2009. According to Gallup, which has tracked public perceptions of unions since 1940, 65 percent of Americans now say they "approve" of unions. That's the highest level since 2000.[19]

It is not just the general public that holds a favorable view of labor unions. Survey evidence reveals that US workers feel inadequately represented in the workplace and desire more influence over working conditions, security, training, and job design, among other job attributes. Task Force member Thomas Kochan and colleagues at the MIT Sloan School of

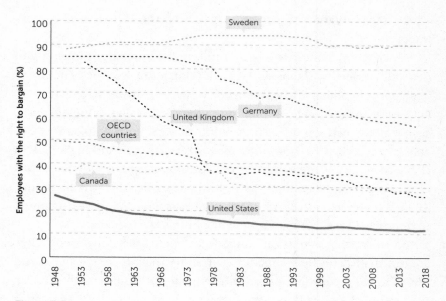

Figure 5.2
Share of Workers Covered by Collective Bargaining in OECD Countries, 1979–2017.
Source: OECD Stat: Collective Bargaining Coverage. ICTWSS database version 6.0
(June 2019).

Management and Columbia University found that a majority of Americans feel they have less influence than they ought to have over a range of workplace issues, including compensation, job security, promotions, respect, and harassment, and over the way new technology is applied to their jobs and in their work organizations more broadly. They define this as a "voice gap." Between one-third and one-half of workers say they also see this gap in other job-related issues, including their employers' values, training, discrimination, the quality of their organization's products or services, and how workplace problems are resolved. The same survey found that worker interest in joining a union has gone up in recent years. Currently, about half of non-unionized workers say they would join a union if given the chance, compared to about one-third who said the same in the 1970s and 1990s. In a follow-up national survey, the authors used an experimental survey design to determine what forms of representation workers prefer. Collective bargaining at the firm or industry level, advising management about employment practices, and worker representation on corporate boards of directors were all cited as important.[20]

The economic rationale for labor unions is subtle but compelling. In perfectly competitive labor markets—the kind found frequently in undergraduate economics textbooks—workers are paid their "marginal product," meaning their net contribution to economic value. Simultaneously, stringent competition drives firm profits to zero. It would be unsustainable in this stylized setting either for workers to command higher wages (since they are already paid their full contribution to economic output) or for firms to share their profits with workers, since there are no profits. There is therefore, in economic theory, no scope for collective bargaining to improve on the free market outcome in this ideal setting.

In reality, labor markets are imperfect in numerous dimensions. They are less than perfectly competitive, meaning that workers may be paid less than their contribution to output while firms may make substantial profits. Alongside these asymmetries of bargaining power, there may be asymmetries of information between firms and workers that allow firms to exploit employees (e.g., blinding them to health and safety hazards) or inhibit employees from voicing their productive ideas and well-founded concerns. Finally, firms may face incentives to make decisions that are profit-maximizing for shareholders but damaging to workers and communities—shuttering plants for the sake of modest private gains with large accompanying social costs, placing workers at unnecessary health and safety risks, or forcing workers to accept exploitative working conditions (e.g., wage theft or willful violations of the law). These deviations from textbook competitive labor market conditions, which many policymakers and economists would agree are commonplace if not universal, create an opportunity for organizations to bargain in good faith on the behalf of workers to negotiate equitable wages and sharing of profits, to reduce information asymmetries that potentially harm workers or firms or both, and to cause firms to recognize and account for some of the social consequences of corporate decisions that are not accounted for by profit and loss statements.

Consistent with this reason, there's strong evidence that unions boost the economic fortunes of their members. As noted by MIT graduate student Gabriel Nahmias, being a union member is estimated to increase

American workers' wages by fifteen to twenty percentage points, while union members are more likely to have such benefits as paid family and medical leave and union shops are associated with narrower racial wage gaps.[21] Research has recognized that the decline of union representation is one of the causes of the failure of wages to rise in tandem with productivity, as they did from the end of World War II through most of the 1970s. Black workers are also overrepresented in labor unions and hence, as with minimum wage, are particularly disadvantaged by the fall in union wage bargaining.[22] Not surprisingly, employers are less enthusiastic about unions than are the workers that unions represent. While there is no definitive evidence as to whether unions hinder or augment employer *productivity*, there is little question that they constrain managerial flexibility (which is never popular with managers) and, if successful, redirect some share of would-be firms' profits into higher worker pay and benefits.

Workers' quest for representation is legitimate—indeed, it is unquestioned in most industrialized countries. Finding a way to improve their representation will require innovation, however. While rebuilding representation can help ensure the gains from technology and other sources of productivity growth flow to improve pay and working conditions, there is likely no one ideal (or widely agreed) model or mechanism for rebuilding worker representation in the workplace.

A challenging but important place for innovation is to implement reforms to the National Labor Relations Act of 1935 (NLRA). The framework provided by the NLRA governing how businesses interact with their workers is unduly restrictive and limits opportunities for cooperative bargaining between worker and employer representatives. In contrast to countries like Germany that mandate worker representation on some company boards and provide work councils that represent workers more broadly, the NLRA makes work councils illegal at nonunion businesses in the US through its ban on company-dominated unions. It is silent on the question of whether workers can serve on corporate boards. The law also excludes agricultural and domestic workers—a legacy of racist attitudes during the New Deal, when southern members of Congress successfully sought to exclude Black workers from new government-mandated protections and benefits. (Blacks made up the overwhelming majority of agricultural and domestic workers in the South at the time.) Despite this history, and distinct from other New Deal legislation that also excluded Black citizens from social protections, the NLRA has not been substantially amended in the eighty-five years since its passage, except by the Taft-Hartley Act in 1947, which weakened the NLRA by restricting some union activities and powers.

Some unions are pushing ahead with significant innovations. For example, UNITE HERE, the union that represents hospitality employees in the hotel, casino, and food service industries, provides an unusual case of negotiations specifically designed to deal with the introduction of new technology. Beginning in 2018, UNITE HERE negotiated agreements with all of the union's major employers for advance notice of up to six months prior to introducing new technology, the right to negotiate about technology with the employer, and the provision of retraining, severance pay, and first consideration for new positions for workers laid off as a result of the new technology. Efforts like this have done little, however, to protect workers from a more basic problem: lack of job security. The massive downturn in travel and leisure amid the pandemic, for instance, sparked massive layoffs.

There is a surge of experimentation with approaches for giving workers a greater voice at work. The Fight for $15 movement has had success in pressing large corporations, including Amazon and Walmart, to raise starting wages even though there are no unions at those companies to coordinate these efforts. The tactics of these groups are often aimed at drawing the attention of consumers to poor working conditions or low pay at large companies. At the beginning of 2021, workers at Google announced they had formed a union (in secret) representing four-hundred-plus engineers and other workers, a rarity at companies with predominantly white-collar workers. Unlike a traditional union, they are a "minority union" representing a small fraction of the company's 260,000 full-time workers and contractors that will not be negotiating for a contract but rather will be a force for change on key issues related to the workplace.

MIT's Nahmias, who studied how the labor movement is experimenting with new forms of collective action, notes that some groups blocked from traditional labor protections have used "secondary labor actions" to pressure employers where they are vulnerable. These groups have developed their own incentives to recruit and maintain members and "have interwoven strategies to help well-intentioned employers to be fair, while sanction[ing] those who refuse to, mixing comprehensive campaigns with strike actions."[23] One of the best-known examples is the United Farm Workers (UFW). Agricultural workers are specifically excluded from protections by the NLRA, but the UFW has found ways to organize tens of thousands of workers—even though it is unable to impose mandatory union dues. The UFW has regularly used secondary boycotts to force large farm businesses to negotiate with them. For example, in 1966 the UAW coordinated a boycott of stores that sold liquor made by farms where UFW workers were striking. Under the NLRA, it's illegal for workers to target the customers of their employers—so this is an example of a group using organizing tools they otherwise would be denied.

Farmworker associations continue to use secondary boycotts. The Coalition of Immokalee Workers, which advocates for farm workers in Florida, has successfully pressured retail companies that sell their produce to pay a few cents per pound to support improvements in farmworkers' wages and benefits.

Many of these new forms of organizing take on broader social issues and don't seek to replicate the model of traditional unions. The National Domestic Workers Alliance (NDWA), founded in 2007, doesn't work to negotiate collective bargaining agreements with employers. Rather it focuses on providing services to its members and advocating for worker rights. The group has seventy-five affiliated organizations and chapters and more than 250,000 members. The NDWA worked along with other organizations to get New York to pass the first state Domestic Worker Bill of Rights in 2010. "Overall, as of October 2020, NDWA has won new rights for domestic workers in nine states and two cities," writes Nahmias. Domestic workers often have multiple employers—which makes it difficult for them to negotiate the terms of their various jobs. The NDWA provides them with tools that help them draft agreements.

The Freelancers Union is an example of groups that also charge no dues and do not negotiate with employers for collective bargaining agreements. Instead, the union negotiates on behalf of its members for better prices on health, dental, and liability insurance. Much like the UFW and NDWA, the Freelancers Union also advocates for laws that benefit its members. For instance, the group was instrumental in passing a New York City law that protects members from clients who refuse to pay for services by mandating contracts, setting required payment terms, and establishing penalties.

Jobs with Justice is a national organization with branches in communities that work on education, research, communication, political action, and projects that promote worker rights. Working Washington is a state-level organization that advocates for workers in that state, including advocating for higher minimum wages and paid sick leave.

To date, none of these models of representation has reached national scale, gained power equivalent to what unions achieved in their heyday through collective bargaining, matched the financial resources associated with major unions, or developed a sustainable business model. Many of them rely on some form of foundation support to cover their costs.

While these alternative models of representation are undergoing rapid evolution, labor law needs to be updated to allow them to flourish as they compete with alternatives. Modernizing labor law is especially important at a time when new technologies and other structural innovations—such as reclassifying more workers as contractors and the rise of app-based businesses such as ridesharing—have made the definition of an "employer" ambiguous.

It is clear that the US needs multiple forms of worker voice and representation that can be tailored to better match the features and needs of different industries, occupational groups, and employment relationships.[24] In keeping with the overall approach of this book to build on existing features of the US labor market system, we conclude that strengthening worker bargaining power requires both strengthening existing labor law and reforming it to be more effective in encompassing the technological and economic changes transforming the workplace and the culture of work. As one example, domestic workers in the US fall outside the scope of the NLRA. But the NLRA's general provisions would be of little use to them even if coverage were available since those provisions are designed to facilitate bargaining between a single employer and its many employees. In domestic work arrangements, however, the relationship is reversed: each domestic worker serves multiple households, so there are many more employers than employees.[25] Analogous issues extend to gig economy work, to independent contracting, to temporary help agency employment, and more broadly to any group of workers that is too dispersed to collectively bargain using conventional means.

CONCLUSION

As in other countries, a growing share of US employment is in traditionally low-paid service jobs: cleaning and groundskeeping, food service, security, entertainment and recreation, and home health assistance. Relative to other high-income countries, however, US workers in these occupations receive extremely low pay and very rarely have access to employer-provided health insurance, family or medical leave, or vacation time. Adjusting for purchasing power, the OECD estimates that low-wage Americans workers are paid 26 percent less than Canadians in similar occupations. It's unlikely that American workers are 26 percent less productive, however. Rather, the combination of low statutory minimum wages, minimal worker representation, and a strong bias toward shareholder primacy in policymaking and corporate governance mean that adequate pay, a modicum of economic security, and access to basic social benefits are not assured for workers on the bottom rungs of the US labor market.

6

INSTITUTIONS FOR INNOVATION

A central lesson from the Task Force's studies of both the economics of the labor market and the current state of technology is how much of new job growth is concentrated in entirely new occupations and industries. Recall that most of today's jobs didn't exist in 1940, and that employment growth in industries like warehousing and distribution is driven by e-commerce, an internet-enabled innovation. The economy depends on new job creation to replenish jobs lost to automation and productivity improvements; the largest and most reliable source of those new jobs are new industries spurred by new technology. To understand how new industries emerge, and how to continue to encourage that emergence, it's important to understand the role of the federal government in investing in new technologies.

THE ROLE OF THE FEDERAL GOVERNMENT IN R&D

In the US, much of that new technology emerges from projects supported by the federal government. Contemporary analysis often focuses on the period since 1940 (see below), but from the earliest days of the republic, the federal government has been an intimate, patient supporter of technology development that created new industries. In the nineteenth century, graduates of the US Military Academy at West Point, America's first engineering school, took the lead in building the nation's railroads and securing national commercial infrastructure. Federal investments in surveying and exploration laid the groundwork for westward expansion, shaped the routes for clipper ships, and suggested paths for transatlantic cables. The Army and Navy bureaus of ordnance and federal armories created interchangeable parts production, seeded the machine tool industry that manufactured guns for the Civil War, and laid the groundwork for the post–Civil War industrial revolutions of typewriters, bicycles, and the mass production of automobiles. The Census Bureau's need for tabulating equipment spurred the innovations of Herman Hollerith that led to the creation of IBM.

Between the world wars, the National Advisory Committee on Aeronautics (NACA), the predecessor to NASA, provided crucial test facilities, data, and skilled personnel to bolster an entirely new industry that was a bulwark of US military and economic power, and a massive source of employment.[1]

Beginning in 1940, this support became more focused, systematic, and innovative. Vannevar Bush, an engineer and inventor who was dean of MIT's School of Engineering in the 1930s, received President Roosevelt's support to create the National Defense Research Committee (NDRC) and its successor the Office of Scientific Research and Development (OSRD), which successfully enlisted scientists and engineers in academia and industry to solve problems for the war effort. Not only did these efforts, such as radar and the Manhattan Project, materially contribute to the war effort, but they drew the map for postwar industry and technology, from miniaturized electronics to penicillin.

Bush's famous 1945 report to the president, *Science, the Endless Frontier,* articulated the vision for how fundamental science could contribute to the economic well-being of the nation through the establishment of the National Science Foundation (NSF). Equally important, however, were the more direct heirs of the OSRD: the Office of Naval Research and then, after Sputnik, DARPA and a host of new federally funded centers such as MIT's Lincoln Lab, national laboratories under the Atomic Energy Commission (later the Department of Energy), R&D efforts internal to the military services, and the creation of NASA out of NACA in 1958. Some of these efforts sponsored technology development geared toward specific agency missions, some funded fundamental research in-house or at universities, and some created large projects for national missions, such as the Apollo program or the Human Genome Project. Even when projects failed to meet their technical goals or technologies languished in a "valley of death" between laboratory and industry, they often created infrastructure, educated technical talent, and seeded ideas and breakthroughs that created the industries of today.

Consider the crucial area of microelectronics: from 1950 to 1970 the federal government funded nearly half of the R&D in the semiconductor industry. The Apollo moon program alone purchased more than half of the integrated circuits produced in the US for several years in the 1960s, giving both commercial boost and technical legitimacy to an unproven technology that went on to transform the economy. Not by coincidence, the microprocessor was invented the year after the Apollo 11 moon landing and found its way into numerous consumer and industrial products.

Equally profound was the federal role in the creation and growth of today's IT, which remains a crucial driver of economic growth and employment a century after its birth. DARPA's Information Processing Technology Office supported the core networking technology and early demonstration network (ARPANET), which became the internet. The agency funded fundamental research in autonomous vehicles, which became the basis for today's autonomous cars, and convened and funded the Grand Challenge competitions that directly created the industry. DARPA-funded research is the basis for today's AI systems, as well as for much of the computer graphics that became the gaming and simulation industries, to name but two examples. Google itself began with a grant from the NSF, and much of the internal components of the iPhone were originally developed with DOD and DOE research funds. Oracle Corporation began with Army-developed database technology.[2]

Similar evidence emerges from the health care and pharmaceutical industries, from new drugs to magnetic resonance imaging machines. The Human Genome Project, funded by the DOE and the National Institutes of Health, not only achieved breakthroughs in genomics but seeded an entire industry of genomic technologies. NIH-funded research underlay every single one of the 210 new drugs approved between 2010 and 2016. Some research indicates the returns on NIH funding to value for private firms on the stock market as three to one, not to mention the employment it generates and the impacts on public health.[3] It would be impossible to mount the rapid response to vaccine development for COVID-19 without a national biomedical research infrastructure built up over many years with federal funding.

Evidence is strong that federal R&D also leads to broad employment benefits. Consider the economic success of regions around major US research universities. In 1980 the Bayh-Dole Act enabled universities to grant exclusive licenses to intellectual property developed with federal dollars, which enhanced their ability to commercialize the technologies developed within their walls. Evidence suggests that these and related policies strongly enhanced the commercial impact of federal R&D dollars, including outside the R&D sector.[4]

Successful federal R&D has been a mix of mission-directed (to solve specific problems, particularly in the military) and fundamental (exploring basic phenomena). Sometimes the government has organized large, mission-directed projects, at other times it has made influential procurements to simply buy what it needed. A recent study found that a third of patent applications for the past century derived from federally funded work, a number that was greater than half in certain industries.[5]

Of course, the federal research record is not perfect. It has had its share of duplication and inefficiency; some government agencies have grown bloated and slow; overall the system failed to address the competitive crisis of the 1980s. Over the years, efforts to tilt the focus more toward commercial development, manufacturing, and regional development have had both successes and failures. Nonetheless, the distributed and overlapping nature of the US federal R&D system is one of its strengths— innovators and good ideas have multiple chances to find support and encouragement. The R&D infrastructure is spread across a broad landscape and has contributed significantly to achieving national goals.

This R&D was not necessarily directed toward industrial applications or job creation, although these benefits have been well documented for a long time. Nonetheless, by focusing on fundamental understanding, fostering experiments, training generations of young innovators, and providing institutional support, federal R&D investments have proved instrumental in both solving national problems and contributing to economic growth—not to mention achieving considerable scientific progress.

Private capital and corporate R&D play crucial roles in bringing new technologies to market, but neither has the consistency or the patience to cultivate the fundamentally new over multiple decades. Indeed, recent research has shown that the majority of the most important new products invented between 1970 to 2006, as identified by *R&D Magazine*'s annual innovation awards, received federal funding at some point during their development from invention to commercialization.[6]

Research by MIT graduate student Daniel Traficonte documents the many advantages and disadvantages to the US R&D system and the important back and forth that has developed between the government and industry in creating a system that generates positive outcomes for society as well as the parties engaged in R&D such as private companies and universities.[7] The positive benefits to society have been estimated to be three to four times as large as the private returns, which bolsters support for additional public R&D investment.[8]

However, as outlined in chapter 2, if the typical worker in the US barely sees or experiences the benefits of increased productivity—generated in part by increases in innovation—we cannot expect to see substantial public support for increased R&D spending. The "great divergence" that began four decades ago and continues today becomes a critical part of the problem that needs to be addressed if we are to adequately invest in the country's innovation capacity for the future.

PRODUCTIVITY, INNOVATION, AND DECLINING FEDERAL INVESTMENT IN R&D

The country's innovation capacity is impressive and has led to innumerable important innovations, due in no small part to the investments by the federal government, as outlined above. But these investments have declined in recent years, raising concerns about the country's ability to continue to sustain its innovation capacity and maintain this crucial national competitive advantage.

The decline in federal research expenditures partly explains the country's lackluster productivity growth rates in the past decade, as outlined in research led by Task Force member Erik Brynjolfsson.[9] The decline is doubly costly because public and private R&D funding are complements: when the government increases its R&D investments, private sector innovation follows; and when the government scales back, the private sector innovates less.[10]

Nobel laureate and Task Force Advisory Board member Robert M. Solow showed decades ago that productivity growth throughout the twentieth century stemmed from technological progress: improvements in tools, techniques, and organizational practices that allowed businesses, households, and government to accomplish more and better work.[11] Many of these technological advances depended in turn on R&D. US public investment in innovation has lagged even as that of other technologically advanced nations has advanced.

US R&D spending overall has declined from 69 percent of the world's R&D spending in 1960 to only 28 percent in 2018.[12] Of course, we would expect this number to decline as other nations have grown wealthier, more educated, and more technologically intensive. But relative to the investments of other leading countries, US investments in R&D have been in decline for at least the past decade.[13] When both public and private R&D investments are combined, Germany invested 2.9 percent of GDP in R&D 2015, versus 2.7 percent in the US and 2.1 percent in China; China in turn is expected to overtake the US and Germany in the years ahead. Japan and South Korea have also surpassed the US with expenditures exceeding 3 percent and 4 percent of GDP, respectively. In addition, even while total US R&D expenditure as a share of GDP has held relatively steady over the last three decades (though has not grown), the public investment share of R&D has fallen steeply over three decades, from approximately 40 percent in 1985 to approximately 25 percent (one quarter) in 2015 (see figure 6.1).

Public R&D expenditure tends to focus on basic science and technologies that may be decades from reaching commercial potential, whereas private R&D expenditure tends to focus on technologies that are closer to market. Accordingly, the adverse effect of declining public R&D effort on innovation is unlikely to be fully offset by the rise in private R&D, even if total expenditures as a share of GDP remain relatively constant.

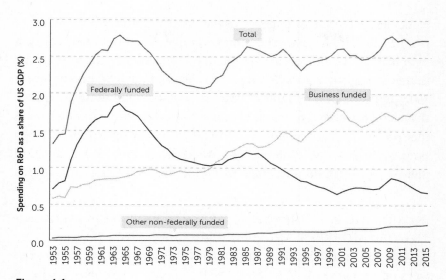

Figure 6.1

US Spending on R&D as a Share of GDP, by Source of Funds, 1953–2015. *Source:* Data from National Science Board, Science and Engineering Indicators 2018. NSB-2018-1, NSF, Alexandria, VA, figure 4.3 (https://www.nsf.gov/statistics/indicators). Original data were drawn from the National Science Foundation, National Center for Science and Engineering Statistics, "National Patterns of R&D Resources" (annual series).

As research by Task Force member Yasheng Huang and graduate student Meicen Sun argues, the Chinese whole-of-government approach to fostering innovation and achieving scale provides an alternative model of all-in innovation.[14] This model is reminiscent of the mega-project approach that the US has favored at various times, including the Manhattan Project, the Apollo program, and the Human Genome Project, but here applied to industrial policy. The whole-of-government approach, however, requires significant political and economic commitment in the US, something that does not come easily to the federal government's highly fragmented and decentralized R&D system.

DIRECTIONS FOR US INNOVATION POLICY AND INSTITUTIONS

Owing to concerns about rising foreign competition, lagging productivity, and growing inequality, leaders across government, business, and

academia are putting forth policy recommendations for ways to reinvigorate US innovation policy and support a more robust industrial policy, a
term that has recently come back into favor. The recent bipartisan legislation proposal, the Endless Frontier Act, harking back to Vannevar Bush's
1945 proposal, is an example of both the ambition and sense of urgency
that exist about the country's innovation trajectory. While we don't detail
the specifics of these proposals, we highlight below several broad directions we believe the US should take where creativity in our innovation
policies and institutions will help create and shape the work of the future.

INCREASING AND DIRECTING FEDERAL RESEARCH SPENDING TOWARD WORKERS AND SOCIETAL CHALLENGES

Federal R&D priorities, in and of themselves, are part of shaping the
work of the future. By identifying the technologically enabled health of
the future US labor market as a national problem worthy of study and
solution by a variety of innovators and researchers, the federal government signals that this is a priority and puts dollars to work for the typical
worker.

Already the NSF has a program titled Future of Work at the Human-
Technology Frontier as one of its ten big ideas for future investments.
The principles of that program offer a template for a broader set of investments, including understanding and advancing human-technology partnerships and promoting technologies to augment human performance.
A further step, not yet taken, would be to establish national research
goals to enhance human capabilities and support equitable labor markets
through research areas such as human-centered AI, collaborative robotics, and the science of learning and education.

Simultaneously, federal research spending should be increased and
directed toward areas that may be neglected by the private sector. Because
of the long payoff horizons and benefits that are hard to monetize, the
private sector faces weak incentives to invest in longer-term, fundamental
research or to support research that would address the social impacts of
technologies. Public investments should focus on technologies and their
application that are needed to solve our most pressing national problems,
including climate change and human health.

Task Force member John Van Reenen makes the case in his brief for the Hamilton Project[15] for a Grand Innovation Fund to support "grand challenges," somewhat like the whole-of-government efforts such as the Apollo moon-shot program or the Human Genome Project. As Van Reenen outlines, the weight of the evidence suggests that industrial policy can have positive impacts on the economy. With the slowdown of growth in the US and the relative success of countries like China with their industrial policies, it is worth a new commitment to "grand challenges" this century. The recent success of Operation Warp Speed in delivering a vaccine for COVID-19 in under a year is an example of what can be achieved when federal R&D dollars and effort are focused on national challenges.

More broadly, the federal government needs to invest in "tough tech,"[16] breakthrough technologies that require more time to mature and often significantly more capital at multiple points in the development cycle. These require patient investment, particularly when it comes to demonstrating viability at scale that requires a level of risk tolerance that is generally unattractive to private sector investors[17]. Examples of such technologies include advanced manufacturing of material and chemicals, next-generation semiconductors, clean energy production and storage, quantum computing, and synthetic biology. Many of these technologies involve a hardware component and unique manufacturing processes, which take more time and funds to develop compared with purely software-based products, where the marginal cost of production approaches zero (though not the first-copy costs). By establishing global expertise and commercialization in new, emerging technologies early on, the US not only benefits economically and invests in its national security, but its inventors, scientists, and policymakers are able to shape the direction of innovation to reflect our values and priorities, including augmenting workers.

Finally, the aftermath of COVID-19 calls for renewed commitments to improve productivity in our small and medium-sized enterprises (SMEs) that face increasing competition from abroad. SMEs represent the majority of our business establishments and are an important part of supply chains, critical to national security, innovation capacity and employment. Supply chain industries are a large and distinct category of the economy, accounting for 43 percent of US private employment in 2015, as research spearheaded by Task Force Advisory Board member Karen Mills has shown. It includes not just manufacturers but also services such as engineering, software, and logistics, industries that have some of the highest wages and intensity of STEM jobs in the US economy.[18]

Ensuring that SME suppliers can compete and innovate in these promising industries will be crucial to creating more of the high-wage, high-technology jobs of the future. As MIT researchers found, many manufacturing suppliers are not making significant investments in new, productivity-enhancing technologies—there are *too few* robots, not too many.[19] To increase productivity among SMEs, we need a renewed commitment to technology investment and upgrading. This could be achieved through federal and state partnerships to subsidize the investment in new equipment or provide guaranteed demand over a period of time for key products, whether defense-related or—as a consequence of what the global pandemic has exposed—in the production of critical health care products.

EXPAND THE GEOGRAPHY OF INNOVATION

Economic inequality has a geographic dimension that has been exacerbated over the past several decades. Regions in the US were converging economically up until the 1980s, but a steady divergence has occurred since then, creating increasing economic disparities between regions as well as within regions, as underscored by the work of author and Task Force co-chair David Autor. Much of this disparity correlates with education levels as well as with population density. Highly-educated, dense cities thrive while nonmetropolitan areas decline. Even within these thriving cities, however, the fortunes of workers without four-year college degrees have stagnated, meaning that regional prosperity doesn't guarantee shared prosperity. Researchers have documented the long lasting economic consequences of regional decline for individuals and indeed, multiple generations, and have suggested several strategies to reverse these trends, or at least slow the decline.[20]

Just as federal R&D investments create positive spillovers effects for the commercial development of new technologies and industries, they also create positive spillovers geographically for those areas that are recipients of these federal dollars. One can hardly calculate the spillovers that come to the Boston region from close to $2 billion per year in federal R&D funding of biotech researchers over the past decade.

Many of the centers of innovation in the US have benefited from increasing returns on their innovation capacity. That is to say, innovation begets more innovation. Silicon Valley's innovation capacity has not leveled off but rather has taken off over the years. Cities that have a high percentage of jobs in innovative industries tend to attract more of these jobs over time.[21] Top innovative cities and regions have become more concentrated, while at the same time more places have become innovation hubs, such as Atlanta, Denver, and Salt Lake City. These trends do not bode well for reducing the concentration of prosperity or the increased income inequality in the country.

To better spread economic opportunity and innovation capacity, researchers and policymakers recommend a geographically informed R&D strategy by the federal government that would bring the employment and economic development benefits of R&D to lagging regions. In recent work, MIT researchers Jonathan Gruber and Simon Johnson outline a strategy in which several regions with some of the essential assets for developing innovation capacity (e.g., a solid percentage of four-year college degree holders, presence of industry) would receive significant federal R&D investments over several years.[22] Experiments with this strategy, as well as others that perhaps work at a smaller scale (such as the industry cluster level) are worthy of investment and could provide important economic benefits to certain places, along with valuable lessons in how to help reverse regional economic decline.

USE OF TAX POLICY TO ENCOURAGE INVESTMENT IN LABOR

Much of the discussion in this book has revolved around whether humans or computers will be cooperating or competing for the jobs of the future. But in one economic arena machines have held a clear advantage over their human counterparts for decades: taxation.

A Task Force brief by MIT professors Daron Acemoglu and Andrea Manera, working with Boston University's Pascual Restrepo, laid out the case in stark percentage terms: "While labor has been taxed at an average rate of about 25 percent for the past four decades, things like equipment, software, and buildings that are classified as capital are taxed at a lower rate—and this rate has fallen steadily in recent years."[23] The average tax rate on software and equipment was just 15 percent in the 1990s and has now dipped to about 5 percent. This differential means that for every dollar workers get in their paychecks, their employer has to pay an additional 25 cents in taxes. For companies, investing that same dollar in capital at a lower rate of taxation, is a much better deal if it can be used effectively to expand output.[24] The issue has grown more urgent as new technologies have made it easier and cheaper to automate jobs across the economy, from warehouses and factories to hospitals and insurance companies. To redress this extreme imbalance, the US should rebalance how it taxes capital and labor to eliminate this built-in bias in favor of capital.

Such a rethink of traditional tax policy is timely, as is shown by earlier research by Acemoglu and Restrepo.[25] The traditional argument for using tax incentives to encourage companies to invest in technology was that, while it might reduce demand for labor, it would also fuel advances in productivity that would create a virtuous cycle of wealth creation that ultimately led to more jobs. This is one reason why investments in technology tend not to reduce the number of jobs available in net. A factory that invests in a new machine might need fewer workers to produce its products, but the advance in productivity that the new machine made possible would frequently stir demand for more products and services, and hence create more jobs.

But this work argues that such policies can encourage companies to invest to reduce their demand for labor without creating that corresponding bump in productivity. Acemoglu and Restrepo have dubbed these "so-so technologies." One example is self-checkout machines at retail stores. The machines reduce the need for cashiers but do little to enhance productivity. Indeed, since an average shopper is probably less skilled at running a checkout than a trained clerk, it likely slows the process. Not that the US should invest less in productive machinery, but let's eliminate cases where automation is being used to replace workers merely because the tax system subsidizes machines.

It is extremely difficult to shape a tax policy that can pick out which technologies will lead to so-so results. It's even difficult to craft policies that distinguish between capital and labor, as clever tax accountants can readily find ways to blur their boundaries. Companies often look for ways to reclassify returns on labor as returns on capital if it allows them to gain a better tax treatment. Hence another strong argument for leveling the tax treatment of labor and capital is that, because the tax system has trouble telling them apart, taxing labor and capital at starkly different rates simply encourages gaming that reduces tax revenue (while enriching the gamers).

One direct step to create a more balanced system would be cut back on depreciation allowances granted to companies. These tax breaks allow companies to almost immediately deduct what they spend on capital investments from their tax bill—deductions that should have occurred over the lifetime of the capital investment. These rapid depreciation allowances were intended to be short-term tools to boost the economy at times of recession. But depreciation allowances have grown much more generous and longer-lasting in recent decades, and companies have lobbied heavily to extend and enhance them.

Another way companies game the tax system is to reclassify themselves as S-corporations in place of conventional C-corporations. Recent work shows that S-corporations are able to more effectively reclassify labor income as capital income, which allows them to enjoy lower effective tax rates.[26] Reducing this asymmetry by placing stricter controls on S-corporations while harmonizing capital and labor taxation would help to address distortion. "These policy actions would broaden the capital income base," write Acemoglu, Manera, and Restrepo, "and that might be enough to bring capital and labor income taxes in line with each other."[27]

The government also offers tax credits for R&D spending to encourage investments in new technologies. These should be maintained given their strong record of success. A close look at the literature found that 1 percent drop in the after-tax price of R&D leads to at least a 1 percent increase in R&D, a rate of return only slightly lower than direct federal funding for research.[28] While keeping the R&D credits in place, the system could be improved by enacting an employer training tax credit. Like the R&D tax credit, this training credit would implicitly have the government share in the cost of employer investments in worker training. Like all tax breaks, this one would need to be tightly regulated to prevent abuses. We would strongly recommend that such a tax break apply only to training that is certified to lead to externally recognized credentials.

It is well known that US has a strong national innovation system, fueled by federal R&D investments, to develop fundamental science and new technologies that has led to scientific leadership and new industries. Less recognized, however, is the crucial link between those new industries as complements to the inevitable loss of jobs that results from productivity enhancing technologies. New industries grew out of a flourishing innovation ecosystem that created new companies and new applications, alongside older industries that increased mechanization and automation as they matured. Yet we have let those important R&D investments lag and potentially wither at a large scale, with corresponding effects on the labor market. Through increased and targeted R&D investments, as well as a tax policy that keeps workers and social challenges at the forefront, the country's innovation system can be put to work for a broader number of people and regions than it has in recent decades.

7

CONCLUSIONS AND POLICY DIRECTIONS

Technological advances are not driving us toward a jobless future. Over the next two decades, industrialized countries will have more job openings than workers to fill them, and robotics and automation will play an increasingly crucial role in closing these gaps. We will ultimately require more technological advances to address humanity's most pressing problems, including climate change, disease, poverty, and inadequate education.

Yet advancing robotics, automation, and as yet unforeseen technologies will not necessarily benefit all workers. These technologies, in concert with economic incentives, policy choices, and institutional forces, will alter the set of jobs available, the quality of the jobs, and the skills they demand. Continuous change challenges us to continually balance innovation, growth and equity.

Most of today's jobs hadn't even been invented in 1940. Inventing new ways of accomplishing existing work, new business models, and entirely new industries drives rising productivity and new jobs. Innovation brings new occupations to life, generates demands for new forms of expertise, and creates opportunities for rewarding work. What human work will look like a century from now is unknown, but most jobs of tomorrow will be distinct from those today, and will owe their existence to the innovations sprouting from scientific and technological progress.

The economic history of the twentieth century shows that a healthy labor market can serve as the foundation for shared prosperity. Well-designed institutions foster opportunity, buttress economic security, and spur democratic participation. The US must commit to rebuilding this foundation in the twenty-first century. It needs to strengthen and build these institutions, launch new investments, and forge policies that ensure that work remains a central, rewarded, esteemed, and economically viable avenue for most adults to prosper.

Three essential pillars support building this more equitable and sustainable economy:

INVEST AND INNOVATE IN SKILLS AND TRAINING

Technological innovation will require workers to have both strong foundational skills and specialized training. Yet the Task Force's research finds that only about half of US workers receive some kind of training from their employers in a given year, and this skews toward higher-educated and nonminority workers. The current US system for training workforce entrants, the currently employed, and displaced workers is fragmented and uneven in quality. It does, however, provide flexibility, which allows workers to move in and out of the system at different points in their careers. Numerous exemplary public, private, and not-for-profit training initiatives exist throughout the country, though some are less successful and most have not been evaluated. Those training models that have been proven successful based on rigorous evaluation should be scaled up to serve many more workers. New technologies, including online instruction, AI-based guided learning systems, and virtual reality tools, offer innovative ways to make training more accessible, affordable, and engaging for students, workers, and job seekers at all stages of the life cycle. To expand and improve pathways to better jobs:

- Foster private sector investment in training, particularly to accelerate upward mobility among lower-wage and less-educated workers, a category in which minority workers are overrepresented. Enact carefully tailored tax code provisions (see above) or matching fund programs to encourage employer-provided training that leads to recognized, verifiable credentials.

- Significantly increase federal funding for training programs that can lead to middle-class jobs for workers without four-year degrees. Support should be offered on a competitive basis to community colleges and labor market intermediaries that can demonstrate they are working closely with employers, providing support services to participants (i.e., coaching, advising, child care, and transportation), and investing in innovative training programs that include work-based learning—elements shown to be keys to success. Encourage the formation of regional compacts formed by employers, governments, community colleges, and community groups that come together with shared commitments to build skill development systems that meet employer needs.

- Support policies that raise degree completion rates at community colleges. Policies should include funding and incentives to redesign the curriculum to integrate (rather than sequence) remedial education and vocational training, create shorter courses that provide usable credentials on the path to a degree, and provide more financial support over shorter intervals to allow adults to focus on studies rather than work while enrolled.

- Require, and fully fund, rigorous evaluations of training programs to gauge efficacy in achieving employment and earnings outcomes.

- Invest in demonstration programs that test innovative ideas for retraining and reemploying dislocated adult workers, a challenge where policy and programs have thus far had limited success.

- Improve labor market information to support workers seeking jobs and jobs seeking workers. Invest in the modernization of traditional "one-stop" centers for unemployed workers while also creating online databases that provide real-time information about job opportunities. Continue to develop ways for workers to easily access to their own data on skills, competencies, and credentials, bearing in mind that job search assistance is a complement to, rather than a substitute for, effective education and training programs.

- Invest in developing and field testing innovative methods and tools for delivering training. Evidence also suggests that online training works best when paired with in-person offerings. Support instructional models that include hands-on learning, potentially using augmented and virtual reality.

IMPROVE JOB QUALITY

As in other countries, a growing share of US employment for workers without four-year college degrees is found in traditionally low-paid service jobs: food service, cleaning and groundskeeping, security, entertainment and recreation, and home health assistance. US workers in these occupations fare worse than in other high-income countries, receiving extremely low pay, irregular schedules, and little or no employment security. They rarely have access to employer-provided health insurance, paid family or medical leave, or vacation time. Adjusting for purchasing power, low-paid Americans are paid 26 percent less than low-paid Canadians. This needn't be the case. The following steps will help to ensure that low-paid jobs provide a modicum of economic security and access to social benefits:

- Restore the real value of the federal minimum wage to at least 40 percent of the national median wage, and index this value to inflation. Localities should be able to set higher levels, as they do currently. Minimum wages are particularly effective at bolstering the earnings of minority workers who are overrepresented at the lower tail of the US wage distribution. The best available economic evidence indicates that well-calibrated minimum wages exert only modest to undetectable adverse effects on employment, but they do reduce household poverty.
- Modernize unemployment insurance (UI) benefits and extend them to workers who have not been traditionally covered:
  - Allow workers to count their most recent earnings toward determining eligibility: At the start of 2019, thirty-seven states allowed workers who did not qualify for benefits using the standard approach to use earnings during a more recent period to establish benefit eligibility. This policy should be adopted nationally.
  - Determine UI eligibility based on hours rather than earnings: At present, low-wage workers must work more hours than high-wage workers to qualify for UI. Already in place in the state of Washington, all states should be required to enable workers to qualify for unemployment benefits by having worked a minimum number of hours rather than having made a minimum level of earnings.

- Drop the requirement that the unemployed seek full-time work: Whether because of family responsibilities or the nature of their jobs, many workers hold part-time positions. Any unemployed worker who searches for part-time work of twenty hours or more per week and who otherwise qualifies for unemployment insurance benefits should be allowed to collect benefits.
- Reform partial UI benefits: States should be required to reevaluate their partial unemployment benefit formulas to better protect workers who lose a substantial fraction of their work hours, including when hours are lost because the worker has lost a second job. In most states, a low-wage worker whose earnings are cut in half would currently receive no benefits.

- Strengthen and adapt labor laws and better enforce them. As private sector labor unions have dwindled, rank-and-file workers have lost the capacity to bargain for wage growth to match productivity growth. Innovation is badly needed in worker representation, but the provisions of US labor law retard the development of alternative approaches. In contrast to the situation in countries like Germany, for example, it is illegal in the US for workers to create work councils at nonunion businesses, and it is unclear whether workers can legally serve on corporate boards.

Key sectors of the workforce, specifically domestic workers and agricultural workers, are excluded from collective bargaining, a legacy of racial politics during the New Deal. The National Labor Relations Act, which has only been amended once in the eighty-five years since its passage (and in that case, to weaken it), requires modernization. The US needs to enable new institutions for collective bargaining to form without undermining the strength of current unions. Action is needed on three fronts:

- Open up labor law to allow innovation in new forms of representation in workplace and corporate decision-making and governance.
- Build legal protections that allow workers to organize without risk of retaliation in nontraditional realms, such as such as domestic and home-care worker, farm work, and independent contracting.
- Strengthen the law and more vigorously enforce protections and processes for workers to gain access to collective bargaining.

EXPAND AND SHAPE INNOVATION

Innovation is key to creating jobs and wealth, and to meeting rising competitive challenges from abroad. The US needs to commit to an innovation agenda that is targeted toward creating social benefits and augmenting rather than replacing workers.

Today, too few of the benefits of innovation-driven growth are flowing to workers. We should steer innovation for the benefit of all stakeholders. Federal policy has clearly been shown to be valuable in seeding innovation, generating economic growth, building areas of educational and research excellence, and spurring new work creation. But publicly directed US innovative effort is slackening, measured either relative to historical levels of public R&D investment or in comparison to effort in other countries, such as Germany and China.

The tax laws that shape corporate investment in workers and machines also need rebalancing. Tax law changes enacted over the last four decades have increasingly skewed the US tax code toward subsidizing machinery purchases rather than investing in workers. Tax policy offers firms an incentive to automate tasks that, absent the distortions of the tax code, they would accomplish with workers. The US should bring its tax code back into balance to align incentives for innovation in skills development, capital formation, and R&D investment. Below is a list of our specific recommendations.

- Increase federal R&D spending and direct it toward areas neglected by the private sector. The private sector faces weak incentives to invest in long-term, fundamental research and to pursue innovations that address the social implications of technologies. Public investments should focus on technologies and applications to solve our most pressing national problems, including climate change, human health, and poverty alleviation.
- Set national research goals to enhance human capabilities and support equitable labor markets through such research areas as human-centered AI, collaborative robotics, and the science of learning and education.
- Offer targeted assistance to SMEs to increase productivity through the adoption of new technologies. Explore ways that federal programs or

departments (e.g., DOD, NIST) could assist in technology upgrading in particular in manufacturing SMEs, possibly through the Manufacturing Extension Partnership and the Manufacturing USA Network.

- Expand the geography of innovation in the US. Innovation is increasingly concentrated geographically. Yet the country has significant assets in its universities, entrepreneurs, and workers that are dispersed throughout the country. With relatively modest amounts of funds and building on existing assets, the US innovation agenda should look to spread the benefits of innovation to a broader set of workers and regions.
- Rebalance taxes on capital and labor by altering the ways the tax code currently unduly favors investments in capital. Eliminate accelerated depreciation allowances, which exacerbate this imbalance.
- Apply the corporate income tax equally to all corporations, including S-corporations. The differential tax treatment of C and S corporations leads to extensive tax arbitrage that relabels labor income as tax-favored capital income. Expanding the tax base is always the most efficient way of raising tax revenue.
- While maintaining the federal R&D tax credit, enact an employer training tax credit, akin to the R&D tax credit, that applies exclusively to training investments in workers that lead to externally recognized certifications.

Too many Americans fear that technological progress will make the country wealthier while threatening their livelihoods.

The remarkable history of American innovation was powered not by fear or fatalism, but by a profound sense of possibility. Those possibilities remain. We see no tradeoff between improving economic security for workers and embracing ongoing technological change and innovation; arguably, accomplishing the latter requires ensuring the former. Achieving both goals will require both technological and institutional innovation.

ACKNOWLEDGMENTS

This book would not have been possible without the committed work of the Task Force and additional contributors from the MIT community. Their valuable participation over the course of two-plus years and contributions to twenty-plus research briefs and the final report represent the foundation and scaffolding of this book. In addition to the Task Force, we would like to thank our Advisory Board and Research Advisory Board for their guidance, insight, and commitment to this effort. A special thank you to Tim Aeppel, our chief editor, for his valuable input into this book from beginning to end, as well as to Sloan graduate student Jihye Gyde for shepherding the book to completion. We'd also like to thank David Goldston, head of the MIT Washington, DC, office, for his excellent contributions to our discussions and reports. Thank you to our Work of the Future team, including Associate Director of the Work of the Future Sarah Jane Maxted, who provided invaluable support to the Task Force; our Communications team, Suzanne Pinto and Stefanie Koperniak; and our excellent administrators, Laura Guild, Anita Kafka, and Jody Gilbert. Finally, we'd like to thank the dozens of students and researchers who were part of a thoughtful, engaging community over the life of the Task Force that generated excellent research and provided valuable insight and support throughout this effort. We are encouraged and inspired by their commitment to ensure their work in the future puts the well-being of workers at the forefront of their contributions to society.

NOTES

1. Josh Cohen, "Good Jobs," MIT Work of the Future Research Brief, RB11-2020.

CHAPTER 2

1. Institutional factors are also essential in determining what technologies are invented, how they are applied, and how they are distributed. See Angus Deaton, *The Great Escape: Health, Wealth, and the Origins of Inequality* (Princeton, NJ: Princeton University Press, 2013).

2. As Moses Finley remarked in a 1973 discussion of the "peculiar institution" of slavery, "In the context of universal history, free labor, wage labor, is the peculiar institution." Moses I. Finley, *The Ancient Economy* (Berkeley: University of California Press, 1973).

3. By more productive, we mean performing the same work at lower total cost. At present, it is infeasible for humans to be more productive than computers in performing standard mathematical calculations, though this was not the case a century ago. Computers are now more productive at this task not only because they are faster but also because they are cheaper than workers at any reasonable wage. The concern is that this will become true in an expanding fraction of all work tasks.

4. The US employment to population ratio has fallen by several percentage points since the year 2000. A substantial driver of this trend is the aging of the US population, which has increased the fraction of adults who are approaching or in retirement. Of course, citizens in high-income countries work fewer annual hours, take more vacations, and retire earlier (relative to age at death) than a century ago—implying that they choose to spend part of their rising incomes on increased leisure. See Stephanie Aaronson, Tomaz Cajner, Bruce Fallick, Felix Galbis-Reig, Christopher L. Smith, and William Wascher, "Labor Force Participation: Recent Developments

and Future Prospects," *Brookings Papers on Economic Activity* 45, no. 2 (2014): 197–275; and David H. Autor, "Why Are There Still So Many Jobs? The History and Future of Workplace Automation," *Journal of Economic Perspectives* 29, no. 3 (2015): 3–30.

5. Though aggregate employment can certainly fall in the short and intermediate term, with substantial adverse consequences for workers. See, for example, Daron Acemoglu and Pascual Restrepo, "Robots and Jobs: Evidence from U.S. Labor Markets," *Journal of Political Economy* 128, no. 6 (2019): 2188–2244.

6. For theoretical analysis and empirical evidence of these ideas, see Daron Acemoglu and Pascual Restrepo, "The Race between Man and Machine: Implications of Technology for Growth, Factor Shares, and Employment," *American Economic Review* 108, no. 6 (2018): 1488–1542; Daron Acemoglu and Pascual Restrepo, "Automation and New Tasks: How Technology Displaces and Reinstates Labor," *Journal of Economic Perspectives* 33, no. 2 (2019): 3–30; and David Autor, Anna Salomons, and Bryan Seegmiller, "New Frontiers: The Origins and Content of New Work, 1940–2018," mimeo, MIT Department of Economics, 2020.

7. To construct this figure, Autor, Salomons, and Seegmiller, in "New Frontiers," use historical data to catalog the introduction of new jobs into the US Census Bureau's occupational coding manuals in each decade between 1940 and 2018.

8. See Daniel P. Gross and Bhaven N. Sampat, "Inventing the Endless Frontier: The Effects of the World War II Research Effort on Post-War Innovation," NBER Working Paper 27375 (Cambridge, MA: National Bureau of Economic Research, 2020); Daniel P. Gross and Bhaven N. Sampat, "Organizing Crisis Innovation: Lessons from World War II," NBER Working Paper 27909 (Cambridge, MA: National Bureau of Economic Research, 2020).

9. See Autor, Salomons, and Seegmiller, "New Frontiers."

10. See Christine Walley, "Robots as Symbol and Social Reality," MIT Work of the Future Research Brief, October 2020.

11. Approximately 60 percent of national income is paid in wages and benefits: Federal Reserve Bank of St. Louis, Economic Research, https://fred.stlouisfed.org/series/LABSHPUSA156NRUG.

12. OAPEC sharply curtailed ("embargoed") oil output in October 1973, ostensibly to punish countries that supported Israel during the 1973 Yom Kippur War. See Daniel Yergin, *The Prize: The Epic Quest for Oil, Money & Power* (New York: Free Press, 2008).

13. The research brief by Task Force member Erik Brynjolfsson along with Seth Benzell and Daniel Rock documents that despite the seeming ubiquity of powerful new technologies with enormous industrial potential, the rate of US productivity growth in recent years has been disappointingly low. US productivity growth averaged 2.8 percent annually between 1995 and 2005, but it has been less than half as rapid since that time. While some have argued that the productivity slowdown is an artifact of measurement, Chad Syverson presents a variety of evidence that mismeasurement is not plausibly large enough to be the main culprit; see Chad Syverson.

"Challenges to Mismeasurement Explanations for the US Productivity Slowdown," *Journal of Economic Perspectives* 31, no. 2 (2017): 165–86. Complementing this conclusion, Brynjolfsson, Benzell, and Rock find that mismeasurement was probably worse *before* the productivity slowdown, meaning mismeasurement only deepens the puzzle; see Erik Brynjolfsson, Seth Benzell, and Daniel Rock, "Understanding and Addressing the Modern Productivity Paradox," MIT Work of the Future Research Brief 13-2020, November 10, 2020.

14. For discussion, see the four articles in "Symposium: The Slowdown in Productivity Growth," *Journal of Economic Perspectives* 4, no. 2 (Fall 1988): 3–97.

15. Reported changes in "real" wage levels should be viewed as approximate; it is not possible to capture all changes in living standards across decades using a single cost of living index. Indeed, the true purchasing power of the median worker has likely risen faster than these numbers suggest, which also means that productivity likely rose faster than depicted here and that real wages stagnated by less. But these caveats do not alter the key points made by figures 2.4 and 2.5: median earnings stagnated relative to productivity growth over the last four decades; earnings of women rose faster than earnings of men; and earnings of whites rose faster than those of Blacks or Hispanics.

16. Edward P. Lazear, "Productivity and Wages: Common Factors and Idiosyncrasies across Countries and Industries," NBER Working Paper 26428 (Cambridge, MA: National Bureau of Economic Research, 2019).

17. See table 2.1 of OECD, "Decoupling of Wages from Productivity: What Implications for Public Policies?," in *OECD Economic Outlook*, vol. 2018, no. 2. The OECD report studies data for the years 1995 through 2013.

18. Wages do not merely reflect productivity, they also determine how productively workers are used. When minimum wages are higher, for example, employers must find ways to make low-paid workers more productive to justify their higher cost. Our argument is not that most wage differentials reflect institutional factors rather than productivity differentials. Rather, we view productivity and wage differentials as a joint outcome of skills investments, technology investments, and institutions. Moreover, skill and technology choices are themselves shaped by institutions and vice versa. For discussion, see Brynjolfsson, Benzell, and Rock, "Understanding and Addressing the Modern Productivity Paradox," and Acemoglu and Restrepo, "The Race between Man and Machine."

19. Florian Hoffmann, David S. Lee, and Thomas Lemieux, "Growing Income Inequality in the United States and Other Advanced Economies," *Journal of Economic Perspectives* 34, no. 4 (2020): 52–78.

20. Marcus Stanley, "College Education and the Midcentury GI Bills," *Quarterly Journal of Economics* 118, no. 2 (2003): 671–708.

21. David Autor, Claudia Goldin, and Lawrence F. Katz, "Extending the Race between Education and Technology," *AEA Papers and Proceedings* 110 (2020): 347–351.

22. In 1979, 60 percent of US males at the median of the wage distribution possessed a high school or lower education, whereas only 20 percent had a bachelor's degree or above. By 2018, fully 35 percent of males at the median of the earnings distribution had attained a four-year college degree—a 75 percent increase—and only one-third had high school or less education. The gain among the median working women was even larger: the four-year degree attainment rate tripled from 13 percent to 45 percent, while the fraction with high school or below dropped from 68 percent to 22 percent. Statistics refer to workers at the forty-fifth to fifty-fifth percentile of the gender-specific hourly wage distribution in the respective year. They are from table 5 of Sarah A. Donovan and David H. Bradley, "Real Wage Trends, 1979 to 2018" (Washington, DC: Congressional Research Service, 2019), 35.

23. See Facundo Alvaredo, Lucas Chancel, Thomas Piketty, Emmanuel Saez, and Gabriel Zucman, eds., *World Inequality Report 2018* (Cambridge, MA: Belknap Press of Harvard University Press, 2018).

24. Brynjolfsson, Benzell, and Rock, "Understanding and Addressing the Modern Productivity Paradox"; Thomas Piketty, Emmanuel Saez, and Stefanie Stantcheva, "Optimal Taxation of Top Labor Incomes: A Tale of Three Elasticities," *American Economic Journal: Economic Policy* 6, no. 1 (2014): 230–271; Josh Bivens and Lawrence Mishel, "The Pay of Corporate Executives and Financial Professionals as Evidence of Rents in Top 1 Percent Incomes," *Journal of Economic Perspectives* 27, no. 3 (2013): 57–78.

25. See Alvaredo et al., *World Inequality Report 2018*. Anglophone countries include Australia, Canada, Ireland, the UK, and the US. Western European countries include France, Germany, Italy, and Spain. Northern European countries include Denmark, Finland, the Netherlands, Norway, and Sweden. The top 1 percent share does not exceed 15 percent in any of these countries and is generally much lower (below 10 percent in Northern Europe). In no other country did it rise by nine percentage points, though the UK comes close to that level.

26. "American Inequality Reflects Gross Incomes as Much as Taxes," *Economist*, April 13, 2019.

27. To be clear, this decline is not due solely to digitalization, as international trade added substantially to the displacement of middle-skilled production and operative jobs during the 2000s. See David H. Autor, David Dorn, and Gordon H. Hanson, "The China Shock: Learning from Labor-Market Adjustment to Large Changes in Trade," *Annual Review of Economics* 8, no. 1 (2016): 205–240.

28. See our discussion of autonomous vehicles in chapter 3 and John Leonard, David Mindell, and Erik Stayton, "Autonomous Vehicles, Mobility, and Employment Policy: The Roads Ahead," MIT Work of the Future Research Brief, July 22, 2020, https://workofthefuture.mit.edu/research-post/autonomous-vehicles-mobility -and-employment-policy-the-roads-ahead.

29. US Bureau of Labor Statistics, Employment Projections, table 1.4: Occupations with the Most Job Growth, 2019 and Projected 2029, https://www.bls.gov/emp /tables/occupations-most-job-growth.htm.

30. The next four occupations on this list are also illustrative: office clerk; executive secretary and executive assistant; inspector, tester, sorter, sampler, and weigher; and bookkeeping, accounting, and auditing clerks.

31. While these projections should be understood as educated guesses, the Bureau of Labor Statistics has a good track record of projecting employment trends at the level of broad occupations. See Andrew Alpert and Jill Auyer, "Evaluating the BLS 1988–2000 Employment Projections," *Monthly Labor Review* (October 2003): 13–37.

32. Because of the nation's aging population, employment in health care occupations is predicted to grow by 18 percent from 2016 to 2026—more than seven times more rapidly than overall employment—and to add 2.4 million jobs. Mercedes Delgado and Karen G. Mills, "The Supply Chain Economy: A New Industry Categorization for Understanding Innovation in Services," *Research Policy* 49, no. 8 (October 2020).

33. Ari Bronsoler, Joseph Doyle, and John Van Reenen, "The Impact of New Technology on the Healthcare Workforce: A White Paper," MIT Work of the Future Research Brief, October 2020.

34. "Measuring and Assessing Job Quality: The OECD Job Quality Framework," In *OECD Social, Employment and Migration Working Papers*, vol. 174, December 18, 2015.

35. For purposes of this comparison, the OECD defines low-skilled workers as those with less than a high school diploma. Performing the same comparison for medium-skilled workers, which the OECD defines as having completed secondary education (i.e., high school), the US ranks tenth among twenty-one countries, where countries eleven through fourteen are the UK, Japan, Finland, and Canada, and countries six through nine are Korea, the Czech Republic, Portugal, and Ireland (https://stats .oecd.org/Index.aspx?QueryId=82334).

36. Jérôme Gautié and John Schmitt, *Low Wage Work in Wealthy Countries* (New York: Russell Sage Foundation, 2009), https://www.russellsage.org/publications/low -wage-work-wealthy-world.

37. Nicholas Kristof, "McDonald's Workers in Denmark Pity Us," *New York Times*, May 8, 2020.

38. In light of the COVID-19 pandemic now sweeping the globe, it bears note that every Dane also has health care and paid sick leave, though these benefits are publicly provided rather than employer-provided, as is typical in the United States.

39. In 2015, only one in six white non-college-educated adults lived in the densest quartile of urban CZs [commuter zones] versus one in four non-college-educated Hispanics and nearly one in three (29 percent) non-college-educated Blacks. In short, many minority workers are situated in the declining urban middle of the US labor market. On a more positive note, Black and Hispanic college graduates are also overrepresented in the densest quartile of urban labor markets. These shares are 34 percent of Hispanic college-degreed workers and 35 percent of Black college-degreed workers versus 26 percent of white college-degreed workers.

40. More encouragingly, among most subgroups of college graduates, polarization was reflected in a rise in employment in both high- and low-paying occupations. An exception to this generalization is the experience of Black male college graduates, however. Their employment share in medium-paying occupations fell by seven percentage points and their share in low-paying occupations rose by almost five percentage points. Thus, despite high levels of educational attainment, they exhibited downward occupational mobility in urban relative to nonurban labor markets. This stark finding is consistent with that of Ellora Derenoncourt , who shows that upward mobility deteriorated among urban Black residents following the Great Migration, and with that of Chetty and co-workers, who document the exceptionally poor labor market outcomes of Black men raised in poor urban US neighborhoods. See Ellora Derenoncourt, "Can You Move to Opportunity? Evidence from the Great Migration," Princeton University Working Paper, December 2019; and Raj Chetty, Nathaniel Hendren, Maggie R. Jones, and Sonya R. Porter. "Race and Economic Opportunity in the United States: An Intergenerational Perspective," *Quarterly Journal of Economics* 135, no. 2 (2020): 711–783.

41. We note that figure 2.9 reports changes in urban relative to nonurban wages by demographic group. The steep decline in the non-college-degreed wage premium could reflect a fall in urban wages among non-college-degreed workers, a rise in nonurban wages among non-college-degreed workers, or a combination of the two.

42. Loukas Karabarbounis and Brent Neiman, "The Global Decline of the Labor Share," *Quarterly Journal of Economics* 129, no. 1 (2014): 61–103.

43. For discussion, see Charles I. Jones and Paul M. Romer, "The New Kaldor Facts: Ideas, Institutions, Population, and Human Capital," *American Economic Journal: Macroeconomics* 2, no. 1 (January 2010): 224–245.

44. This argument is made most forcefully in Thomas Philippon, *The Great Reversal: How America Gave Up on Free Markets* (Cambridge, MA: Belknap Press of Harvard University Press, 2019).

45. For evidence on the relationship between rising market power and the declining labor share, see Jan De Loecker, Jan Eeckhout, and Gabriel Unger, "The Rise of Market Power and the Macroeconomic Implications," *Quarterly Journal of Economics* 135, no. 2 (January 23, 2020): 561–644.

46. Philippon, *The Great Reversal*, argues that most countries have *not* relaxed their antitrust policies and disputes that labor shares have fallen in most countries. For evidence on the latter point, see Germán Gutiérrez and Sophie Piton, "Revisiting the Global Decline of the (Non-Housing) Labor Share," *American Economic Review: Insights* 2, no. 3 (2020): 321–338.

47. See Michael W. L. Elsby, Bart Hobijn, and Ayşegül Şahin, "The Decline of the U.S. Labor Share," *Brookings Papers on Economic Activity* 2013, no. 2 (2013): 1–63.; David Autor and Anna Salomons, "Is Automation Labor Share-Displacing? Productivity Growth, Employment, and the Labor Share," *Brookings Papers on Economic Activity* 2018, no. 1 (2018): 1–87; and Acemogluand Restrepo, "Robots and Jobs."

48. Daron Acemoglu, Claire LeLarge, and Pascual Restrepo, "Competing with Robots: Firm-Level Evidence from France," NBER Working Paper 26738 (Cambridge, MA: National Bureau of Economic Research, February 2020).

49. This finding is reported in two recent papers: David Autor, David Dorn, Lawrence F. Katz, Christina Patterson, and John Van Reenen, "The Fall of the Labor Share and the Rise of Superstar Firms," *Quarterly Journal of Economics* 135, no. 2 (May 1, 2020): 645–709; and Matthias Kehrig and Nicolas Vincent, "The Micro-Level Anatomy of the Labor Share Decline," NBER Working Paper 25275 (Cambridge, MA: National Bureau of Economic Research, rev. October 2020).

50. Abhijit V Banerjee and Esther Duflo, "Inequality and Growth: What Can the Data Say?," *Journal of Economic Growth* 8, no. 3 (2003): 267–299.

51. Raj Chetty, David Grusky, Maximilian Hell, Nathaniel Hendren, Robert Manduca, and Jimmy Narang, "The Fading American Dream: Trends in Absolute Income Mobility Since 1940," *Science* 356, no. 6336 (2017): 398–406.

52. The corresponding figures for the UK and Denmark are 9 percent and 11.7 percent, respectively.

53. Lawrence F. Katz and Alan B. Krueger, "Documenting Decline in U.S. Economic Mobility," *Science* 356, no. 6336 (2017): 382–383, https://doi.org/10.1126/science.aan 3264.

54. Bart Van Ark, Mary O'Mahoney, and Marcel P. Timmer, "The Productivity Gap between Europe and the United States: Trends and Causes," *Journal of Economic Perspectives* 22, no. 1 (2008): 25–44, https://www.aeaweb.org/articles?id=10.1257/jep.22.1.25.

55. Brynjolfsson, Benzell, and Rock, "Understanding and Addressing the Modern Productivity Paradox."

56. Philippe Aghion, Ufuk Akcigit, Antonin Bergeaud, Richard Blundell, and David Hemous, "Innovation and Top Income Inequality," *Review of Economic Studies* 86, no. 1 (2019): 1–45.

57. Indeed, one could make a stronger argument: It is necessary to preserve opportunity and economic mobility for the vast majority of citizens to maintain the public consensus on which a democratic free market system stands.

58. Brynjolfsson, Benzell, and Rock, "Understanding and Addressing the Modern Productivity Paradox."

59. David Autor, David Dorn, Gordon Hanson, and Kaveh Majlesi, "Importing Political Polarization? The Electoral Consequences of Rising Trade Exposure," *American Economic Review* 110, no. 10 (2020): 3139–3183.

60. Barry Naughton, *The Chinese Economy: Transitions and Growth* (Cambridge, MA: MIT Press, 2007).

61. For further evidence that institutional differences play a key role in inequality among median- and below-median-wage workers, see Stijn Broecke, Glenda Quintini, and Marieke Vandeweyer, "Wage Inequality and Cognitive Skills: Reopening the Debate," in *Education, Skills, and Technical Change: Implications for Future US GDP*

Growth, ed. Charles R. Hulten and Valerie A. Ramey, vol. 77 of *Studies in Income and Wealth* (Chicago: University of Chicago Press, 2018).

62. Lawrence Mishel, Lynn Rhinehart, and Lane Windham, "Explaining the Erosion of Private-Sector Unions," Economic Policy Institute, October 2020.

63. See David H. Autor, Alan Manning, and Christopher L. Smith, "The Contribution of the Minimum Wage to US Wage Inequality over Three Decades: A Reassessment," *American Economic Journal: Applied Economics* 8, no. 1 (2016): 58–99; Doruk Cengiz, Arindrajit Dube, Attila Lindner, and Ben Zipperer. "The Effect of Minimum Wages on Low-Wage Jobs," *Quarterly Journal of Economics* 134, no. 3 (2019): 1405–1454; Ellora Derenoncourt and Claire Montialoux, "Minimum Wages and Racial Inequality," *Quarterly Journal of Economics* 136, no. 1 (2021): 169–228; and Ellora Derenoncourt, and Claire Montialoux, "Opinion: To Reduce Racial Inequality, Raise the Minimum Wage," *New York Times*, October 25, 2020.

64. David Weil, *The Fissured Workplace: Why Work Became So Bad for So Many and What Can Be Done to Improve It* (Cambridge: Harvard University Press. 2014).

65. See Christine Walley, "Robots as Symbol and Social Reality," MIT Work of the Future Research Brief 10-2020, October 29, 2020; Steven Greenhouse, *Beaten Down, Worked Up: The Past, Present, and Future of American Labor* (New York: Knopf, 2019).

CHAPTER 3

1. Christine J. Walley, "Robots as Symbols and Social Technology," MIT Work of the Future Research Brief 10-2020, October 29, 2020.

2. Thomas M. Malone, Daniela Rus, and Robert Laubacher, "Artificial Intelligence and the Future of Work," MIT Work of the Future Research Brief 17-2020, December 17, 2020.

3. Ari Bronsoler, Joseph Doyle, and John Van Reenen, "The Impact of New Technology on the Healthcare Workforce," MIT Work of the Future Research Brief 09-2020, October 26, 2020.

4. Erik Brynjolfsson, Seth Benzell, and Daniel Rock, "Understanding and Addressing the Modern Productivity Paradox," MIT Work of the Future Research Brief 13-2020, November 10, 2020.

5. Malone, Rus, and Laubacher, "Artificial Intelligence and the Future of Work."

6. Rodney Brooks, "Steps toward Super Intelligence II, Beyond the Turing Test," [FoR&AI] (blog), July 15, 2018, https://rodneybrooks.com/forai-steps-toward-super-intelligence-ii-beyond-the-turing-test.

7. Elisabeth Reynolds and Anna Waldman-Brown, "Digital Transformation in a White-Collar Firm: Implications for Workers across a Continuum of Jobs and Skills," MIT Work of the Future Working Paper, 2021.

8. Bronsoler, Doyle, and Van Reenen, "The Impact of New Technology on the Healthcare Workforce."

9. Paul Osterman, *Who Will Care for Us? Long-Term Care and the Long-Term Workforce* (New York: Russell Sage Foundation, 2017).

10. Margot Sanger-Katz, "Why 1.4 Million Health Jobs Have Been Lost during a Huge Health Crisis," *New York Times,* May 10, 2020, B4.

11. Nicholas Bloom, Renata Lemos, Raffaella Sadun, and John Van Reenen, "Healthy Business? Managerial Education and Management in Health Care," *Review of Economics and Statistics* 102, no. 3 (2020): 506–517.

12. Richard Hillestad, James Bigelow, Anthony Bower, Federico Girosi, Robin Meili, Richard Scoville, and Roger Taylor, "Can Electronic Medical Record Systems Transform Health Care? Potential Health Benefits, Savings, and Costs," *Health Affairs* 24, no. 5 (2005): 1103–1117.

13. Arthur L. Kellermann and Spencer S. Jones, "What It Will Take to Achieve the As-Yet-Unfulfilled Promises of Health Information Technology," *Health Affairs* 32, no. 1 (2013): 63–68.

14. Zeng Xiaoming, "The Impacts of Electronic Health Record Implementation on the Health Care Workforce," *North Carolina Medical Journal* 77, no. 2 (2016): 112–114.

15. John J. Leonard, David A. Mindell, and Erik L. Stayton, "Autonomous Vehicles, Mobility, and Employment Policy: The Roads Ahead," MIT Work of the Future Research Brief 02-2020, July 22, 2020, https://workofthefuture.mit.edu/research-post/autonomous-vehicles-mobility-and-employment-policy-the-roads-ahead.

16. For a review of recent models that estimate the adoption of EVs and their impact on jobs, see Anuraag Singh, "Modeling Technological Improvement, Adoption, and Employment Effects of Electric Vehicles: A Review," MIT Work of the Future Working Paper, forthcoming, http://dx.doi.org/10.2139/ssrn.3859496.

17. Leonard, Mindell, and Stayton, "Autonomous Vehicles, Mobility, and Employment Policy."

18. Erica L. Groshen, Susan Helper, John Paul MacDuffie, and Charles Carson, "Preparing U.S. Workers and Employers for an Autonomous Vehicle Future" (Kalamazoo, MI: W. E. Upjohn Institute, June 1, 2018).

19. David A. Mindell, *Our Robots, Ourselves: Robotics and the Myths of Autonomy* (New York: Viking Penguin, 2015).

20. See Russell Glynn, Mario Goetz, and Kevin X. Shen, "Avenues of Institutional Change: Technology and Urban Mobility in Southeast Michigan," MIT Work of the Future Working Paper 08-2020, December 11, 2020.

21. Glynn, Goetz, and Shen, "Avenues of Institutional Change."

22. Arshia Mehta and Frank Levy, "Warehousing, Trucking, and Technology: The Future of Work in Logistics," MIT Work of the Future Research Brief, September 8, 2020, https://workofthefuture.mit.edu/research-post/warehousing.

23. Mehta and Levy, "Warehousing, Trucking, and Technology."

24. Bridget McCrea, "Reader Survey: There's No Stopping Warehouse Automation," Logistics Management, July 23, 2020, https://www.logisticsmgmt.com/article/theres_no_stopping_warehouse_automation_covid_19.

25. Mehta and Levy, "Warehousing, Trucking, and Technology."

26. Formally, this would imply that the product has changed, not that productivity per se has fallen: warehousing firms have not gotten worse at what they traditionally do, but they are now asked to do something harder.

27. Mehta and Levy, "Warehousing, Trucking, and Technology."

28. Lindsay Sanneman, Christopher Fourie, and Julie Shah, "The State of Industrial Robotics: Emerging Technologies, Challenges and Key Research Directions," MIT Work of the Future Research Brief, RB15-2020.

29. Sanneman, Fourie, and Shah, "The State of Industrial Robotics," 28.

30. Susan Helper, Elisabeth Reynolds, Daniel Traficonte, and Anuraag Singh. "Factories of the Future: Technology, Skills, and Innovation at Large Manufacturing Firms," MIT Work of the Future Research Brief, 2021.

31. Susan Helper, Raphael Martins, and Robert Seamans, "Who Profits from Industry 4.0? Theory and Evidence from the Automotive Industry," SSRN Electronic Journal, January 2019, 10.2139/ssrn.3377771.

32. Helper, Reynolds, Traficonte, and Singh, "Factories of the Future," 4.

33. Suzanne Berger, Lindsay Sanneman, Daniel Traficonte, Anna Waldman-Brown, and Lukas Wolters, "Manufacturing in America: A View from the Field," MIT Work of the Future Research Brief, 2020.

34. Sanneman, Fourie, and Shah, "The State of Industrial Robotics."

35. Anna Waldman-Brown, "Redeployment or Robocalypse? Workers and Automation in Ohio Manufacturing SMEs," Cambridge Journal of Regions, Economy and Society 13, no. 1, (2020): 99–115.

36. Haden Quinlan and John Hart, "Additive Manufacturing: Implications for Technological Change, Workforce Development, and the Product Lifecycle," MIT Work of the Future Research Brief, November 2020.

37. In economic terms, this depends on whether demand for industry output is elastic or inelastic—that is, whether a fall in price generates a more than or less than proportionate increase in demand.

CHAPTER 4

1. David Autor, "Skills, Education, and the Rise of Earnings Inequality among the 'Other 99 percent,'" Science 344, no. 6186 (2014): 843–851.

2. David Autor, David Mindell, and Elisabeth Reynolds, "The Work of the Future: Building Better Jobs in an Age of Intelligent Machines," MIT Work of the Future, 2020.

3. Christopher Avery and Sarah Turner (2012). Student Loans: Do College Students Borrow Too Much—Or Not Enough? *Journal of Economic Perspectives* 26, no. 1 (2012): 165–192.

4. Seth D. Zimmerman, "The Returns to College Admission for Academically Marginal Students," *Journal of Labor Economics* 32, no. 4 (2014): 711–754.

5. Unfortunately, the historical Current Population Survey data used to construct figure 2.2 do not, for most of the relevant time period, distinguish between two-year degree holders and those who attended a two- or four-year college program but did not attain a degree. This inadvertent mixing of categories may mask some of the earnings benefits associated with two-year degree completion.

6. Clive Belfield and Thomas Bailey, "The Labor Market Returns to Sub-Baccalaureate College: A Review. A CAPSEE Working Paper" (New York: Center for Analysis of Postsecondary Education and Employment, 2017).

7. Anne Huff Stevens, Michal Kurlaender, and Michel Grosz. "Career Technical Education and Labor Market Outcomes: Evidence from California Community Colleges." *Journal of Human Resources*, 54, no. 4 (2019): 986–1036; Christopher Jepsen, Kenneth Troske, and Paul Coomes, "The Labor-Market Returns to Community College Degrees, Diplomas, and Certificates," *Journal of Labor Economics* 32, no. 1 (2014): 95–121.

8. As explained in Jepsen, Troske, and Coomes, "The Labor-Market Returns," "Community colleges are diverse institutions that offer several opportunities for individuals to gain human capital. Community colleges offer a variety of each of the three types of awards: degrees, diplomas, and certificates. Certificates are primarily awarded in technical programs and typically require one or two semesters of course work. Examples include medical records coding specialist, IT network administrator, automotive mechanic, and electrician. Diplomas typically require more than a year of study and are also most common in technical fields, such as surgery technology, accounting, and practical nursing. Associate's degrees require the most number of credits, 60–76, depending on the field of study. The curricula for associate's degree programs have much in common with those of the first 2 years of a 4-year college, including liberal arts and general education courses as well as those geared to specific vocations, such as registered nursing. Associate's degree credits generally are transferrable to a 4-year college toward a bachelor's degree."

9. Stevens, Kurlaender, and Grosz, "Career Technical Education and Labor Market Outcomes."

10. This next section draws heavily from Lawrence F. Katz, Jonathan Roth, Richard Hendra, and Kelsey Schaberg, "Why Do Sectoral Employment Programs Work? Lessons from WorkAdvance," NBER Working Paper 28248 (Cambridge, MA: National Bureau of Economic Research, December 2020).

11. See David Deming, "The Growing Importance of Social Skills in the Labor Market," *Quarterly Journal of Economics* 132, no. 4 (2017): 1593–1640.

12. See Paul Osterman, "Skill Training for Adults," MIT Work of the Future Research Brief, 2020

13. See Thomas J. Kane and Cecilia E. Rouse, "Labor-Market Returns to Two- and Four-Year College: Is a Credit a Credit and Do Degrees Matter?," *American Economic Review* 85, no. 3 (1995): 600–614; and Christopher Jepsen, Kenneth Troske, and Paul Coomes. "The Labor-Market Returns to Community College Degrees, Diplomas, and Certificates," *Journal of Labor Economics* 32, no. 1 (January 1, 2014): 95–121.

14. Susan Scrivener, Michael J. Weiss, Alyssa Ratledge, Timothy Rudd, Colleen Sommo, and Hannah Fresques, "Doubling Graduation Rates: Three-Year Effects of CUNY's Accelerated Study in Associate Programs (ASAP) for Developmental Education Students," SSRN Scholarly Paper (Rochester, NY: Social Science Research Network, 2015).

15. Eli Zimmerman, "Major Companies Partner with Colleges for Education Opportunities in Emerging Tech," *EdTech: Focus on Higher Education*, 2018.

16. M. Cormier, L. Pellegrino, T. Brock, H. Glatter, R. Kazis, and J. Jacobs, "Automation and Technological Changes in the Workplace: Implications for Community College Workforce Training Programs," Columbia University, Teachers College, Community College Research Center, forthcoming.

17. Osterman, "Skill Training for Adults."

18. Katz, Roth, Hendra, and Schaberg, "Why Do Sectoral Employment Programs Work?"

19. See Marianne Bertrand, Magne Mogstad, and Jack Mountjoy, "Improving Educational Pathways to Social Mobility: Evidence from Norway's 'Reform 94'" (*Journal of Labor Economics*, forthcoming), for a discussion about high school vocational education: it has a controversial history in the United States, largely because of a perceived trade-off between teaching readily deployable occupational skills versus shunting mostly disadvantaged students away from the educational and career flexibility afforded by general academic courses.

20. For examples of this and other new delivery models, see William B. Bonvillian, Sanjay Sarma, Meghan Perdue, and Jenna Myers, *The Workforce Education Project Preliminary Report*, MIT Office of Open Learning, April 2020.

21. Robert Lerman, "Scaling Apprenticeships to Increase Human Capital," in *Expanding Economic Opportunity for More Americans*, ed. Melissa Kearney and Amy Ganz (Washington, DC: Aspen Institute, February, 2019), 56–75.

22. Kathleen Thelen and Christian Lyhne Ibsen, "Growing Apart: Efficiency and Equality in the German and Danish VET Systems," MIT Work of the Future Research Brief, October 2020.

23. US Department of Education, National Center for Education Statistics, "Post-Secondary Institution Expenses," May 2020, https://nces.ed.gov/programs/coe/indicator_cue.asp.

24. For details on this example and additional overview of the US workforce education and training system and emerging delivery models, see William B. Bonvillian and Sanjay E. Sarma, *Workforce Education: A New Roadmap* (Cambridge, MA: MIT Press, 2021).

25. For details about the FCA, see the following news article: Breana Noble, "FCA Has Hired 4,100 Detroit Residents for Its New Detroit Assembly Complex," *Detroit News*, October 21, 2020, https://www.detroitnews.com/story/business/autos/chrysler /2020/10/21/detroiters-filling-half-available-jobs-fcas-new-assembly-plant/6004528 002.

26. For a review of these programs, see Osterman, "Skill Training for Adults."

27. See A. Clochard-Bossuet and G. Westerman, "Understanding the Incumbent Workers' Decision to Train: The Challenges Facing Less Educated Workers," MIT Work of the Future Working Paper, 2020.

28. Fei Qin and Thomas Kochan, "The Learning System at IBM: A Case Study," draft report, MIT Sloan School of Management, December 2020.

29. For references related to this section, see Osterman, "Skill Training for Adults.".

30. Paul Osterman, "How Americans Obtain Their Work Skills," MIT Sloan School Working Paper, 2020.

31. For an example of multistate collaboration around skills development across stakeholders, see the website of the Greater Washington Partnership at http://www .greaterwashingtonpartnership.com.

32. For more examples of worker-supporting regional partnerships, including their use of employer engagement techniques to shape technological change in the workplace, see Nichola Lowe, *Putting Skill to Work: How to Create Good Jobs in Uncertain Times* (Cambridge, MA: MIT Press, 2021).

33. Manufacturing Extension Partnership, utilizing an online survey of the MEP national network as well as focus groups, which concluded that credentials are "not routinely required or used" by firms. These results are consistent with a nationally representative survey conducted in 2012 and 2013 that found that only 7.4 percent of manufacturing firms responded affirmatively to the question, "Do you use any formal industry skill credentials system, such as those provided by industry associations or national testing services, for hiring core employees?" See Osterman, "Skill Training for Adults."

34. The US Chamber of Commerce Foundation has recently put forth a proposal for Learning and Experience Records. See US Chamber of Commerce, American Workforce Policy Advisory Board web page at https://www.commerce.gov/american worker/american-workforce-policy-advisory-board.

35. Alistair Fitzpayne and Ethan Pollack, "Lifelong Learning and Training Accounts: Helping Workers Adapt and Succeed in a Changing Economy" (New York: Aspen Institute Future of Work Initiative, May 2018), 1–12.

36. David J. Deming, Claudia Goldin, and Lawrence F. Katz, "The For-Profit Postsecondary School Sector: Nimble Critters or Agile Predators?," *Journal of Economic Perspectives* 26, no. 1 (2012): 139–164; David J. Deming, Noam Yuchtman, Amira Abulafi, Claudia Goldin, and Lawrence F. Katz. "The Value of Postsecondary Credentials in the Labor Market: An Experimental Study," *American Economic Review* 106, no. 3 (2016): 778–806.

37. Doug Lederman, "Online Is (Increasingly) Local," *Inside Higher Ed*, June 5, 2019, https://www.insidehighered.com/digital-learning/article/2019/06/05/annual-sur vey-shows-online-college-students-increasingly?utm_source=naicu.

38. Dhawal Shah, "Year of MOOC-Based Degrees: A Review of MOOC Stats and Trends in 2018," Class Central, January 6, 2019, https://www.classcentral.com /report/moocs-stats-and-trends-2018.

39. Sanjay Sarma and William B. Bonvillian, "Applying New Education Technologies to Meet Workforce Education Needs," MIT Work of the Future Research Brief, October 2020.

CHAPTER 5

1. See the final report of the Work of the Future Task Force: David Autor, David A. Mindell, and Elisabeth B. Reynolds, "The Work of the Future: Building Better Jobs in an Age of Intelligent Machines," MIT Work of the Future, 2020, figure 7.

2. Tavneet Suri, "Universal Basic Income: What Do We Know?," MIT Work of the Future Research Brief, 2020.

3. Katharine G. Abraham, Susan Houseman, and Christopher J. O'Leary, "Extending Unemployment Insurance Benefits to Workers in Precarious and Nonstandard Arrangements," MIT Work of the Future Research Brief, November 2020.

4. Chris O'Leary and Stephen A. Wandner, "An Illustrated Case for Unemployment Insurance Reform," Upjohn Institute Working Paper 19-317, 2020.

5. The following groups of workers are entirely exempted from the federal minimum wage: (1) white-collar employees, (2) farmworkers employed on small farms, (3); seasonal recreational employees, and (4) companions for the elderly. The following groups of workers may be paid a subminimum wage: (1) workers with disabilities, (2) full-time students, (3) employees under twenty years old in their first ninety consecutive days of employment, (4) tipped employees, (5) student learners, (6) apprentices, and (7) messengers. At present, the federal minimum nontipped wage is $7.25 per hour while the tipped wage is $2.13 per hour. See US Department of Labor, "Questions and Answers about the Minimum Wage," https://www.dol .gov/agencies/whd/minimum-wage/faq.

6. Doruk Cengiz, Arindrajit Dube, Attila Lindner, and Ben Zipperer, "The Effect of Minimum Wages on Low-Wage Jobs," *Quarterly Journal of Economics* 134, no. 3 (2019): 1405–1454.

7. We do not specify a number here, but research offers guidance on this choice. See Arindrajit Dube, "Impacts of Minimum Wages: Review of the International Evidence," report prepared for Her Majesty's Treasury (UK), November 2019.

8. Daniel Aaronson, "Price Pass-Through and the Minimum Wage," *Review of Economics and Statistics* 83, no. 1 (2001): 158–169; Christian Dustmann, Attila Lindner, Uta Schönberg, and Matthias Umkehrer, "Reallocation Effects of the Minimum Wage," CReAM Discussion Paper CDP 07/20 (London: Centre for Research and Analysis of Migration, University College London, February 2020).

9. The federal Family and Medical Leave Act of 1993 requires covered employers (generally businesses with more than fifty employees) to provide employees with job-protected, *unpaid* leave for qualified medical and family reasons.

10. In its ranking of the economic security of low-wage workers, the OECD in 2015 ranked the US at number twenty-two of twenty-nine countries. The most secure countries in the list were Luxembourg, Korea, and Austria; the least secure were Latvia, Estonia, and the Slovak Republic. The only two Western European countries ranked below the US were Ireland and Spain, at numbers twenty-three and twenty-four (see https://stats.oecd.org/Index.aspx?QueryId=82334).

11. Paul Osterman, *Who Will Care for Us? Long-Term Care and the Long-Term Workforce* (New York: Russell Sage Foundation, 2017).

12. See US Bureau of Statistics, "Home Health and Personal Care Aides" and "Nursing Assistants and Orderlies" in *Occupational Outlook Handbook*, https://www.bls.gov/ooh/healthcare/home-health-aides-and-personal-care-aides.htm and https://www.bls.gov/ooh/healthcare/nursing-assistants.htm.

13. See "In Advanced and Emerging Economies Alike, Worries about Job Automation," *Global Attitudes & Trends Project* (blog), Pew Research Center, September 13, 2018, https://www.pewresearch.org/global/2018/09/13/in-advanced-and-emerging-economies-alike-worries-about-job-automation.

14. Business Roundtable, "Statement on the Purpose of a Corporation," August 2019, https://opportunity.businessroundtable.org/wp-content/uploads/2019/08/Business-Roundtable-Statement-on-the-Purpose-of-a-Corporation-with-Signatures.pdf.

15. Ellora Derenoncourt, Clemens Noelke, and David Weil, "Spillover Effects from Voluntary Employer Minimum Wages," paper presented at NBER Labor Studies Summer Institute, July 2020.

16. Paul Osterman, "In Search of the High Road: Meaning and Evidence," *ILR Review* 71, no. 1 (January 2018): 3–34.

17. Binyamin Appelbaum, "50 Years of Blaming Milton Friedman. Here's Another Idea," *New York Times*, September 18, 2020, sec. Opinion.

18. See, for example, James A. Schmitz Jr., "What Determines Productivity? Lessons from the Dramatic Recovery of the US and Canadian Iron Ore Industries Following Their Early 1980s Crisis," *Journal of Political Economy* 113, no. 3 (June 2005): 582–625.

19. Pew survey data from 2018 find that 51 percent of Americans view the long-term decline in union membership as mostly bad, while 35 percent view it as mostly good. Among those who lean toward the Democratic Party, those shares are 68 percent negative and 21 percent positive. Among those who lean Republican, the shares are 53 percent positive and 34 percent negative. Hannah Fingerhut, "More Americans View Long-Term Decline in Union Membership Negatively Than Positively," *FactTank* (blog), Pew Research Center, June 5, 2018, https://www.pewresearch.org/fact-tank/2018/06/05/more-americans-view-long-term-decline-in-union-membership-negatively-than-positively.

20. Thomas A. Kochan, Duanyi Yang, William T. Kimball, and Erin L. Kelly, "Worker Voice in America: Is There a Gap between What Workers Expect and What They Experience?," *ILR Review* 72, no. 1 (2019): 3–38; Alexander Hertel-Fernandez, William T. Kimball, and Thomas A. Kochan, "What Forms of Representation Do American Workers Want? Implications for Theory, Policy, and Practice," *ILR Review*, September 2020.

21. Gabriel Nahmias, "Innovations in Collective Action in the Labor Movement: Organizing Workers beyond the NLRA and the Business Union," Work of the Future Working Paper No. 13, 2021.

22. In 2018, 13.8 percent of Black versus 11.5 percent of white workers were represented by a union. Conversely, only 10.1 percent of Hispanic workers had union representation. See BLS Economic News Release: Union Members Survey, 1/22/2020, table 1, https://www.bls.gov/news.release/union2.nr0.htm.

23. Nahmias, "Innovations in Collective Action in the Labor Movement."

24. Thomas Kochan, "Worker Voice, Representation, and Implications for Public Policies," MIT Work of the Future Research Brief, July 8, 2020, 2, https://workoft -hefuture.mit.edu/research-post/worker-voice-representation-and-implications-for -public-policies.

25. The NLRA has specific provisions to encourage collective bargaining in labor markets where the employer-employee relationship is neither permanent nor exclusive, but these provisions are limited to the construction sector.

CHAPTER 6

1. A. Hunter Dupree, *Science in the Federal Government: A History of Policies and Activities to 1940* (Cambridge, MA: Belknap Press of Harvard University Press, 1957); Merritt Roe Smith, *Harpers Ferry Armory and the New Technology: The Challenge of Change* (Ithaca, NY: Cornell University Press, 2015); Alfred D. Chandler, *The Visible Hand: The Managerial Revolution in American Business* (Cambridge, MA: Belknap Press of Harvard University Press, 1977); David Hounshell, *From the American System to Mass Production, 1800–1932: The Development of Manufacturing Technology in the United States* (Baltimore, MD: Johns Hopkins University Press, 1985).

2. National Research Council, *Funding a Revolution: Government Support for Computing Research.* (Washington, DC: National Academy Press, 1999); Alex Roland and Philip Shiman, *Strategic Computing: DARPA and the Quest for Machine Intelligence, 1983–93* (Cambridge, MA: MIT Press, 2002); Arthur Norberg, Judy O'Neill, and Kerry Freedman, *Transforming Computer Technology: Information Processing for the Pentagon* (Baltimore, MD: Johns Hopkins University Press, 1996); Mariana Mazzucato, *The Entrepreneurial State: Debunking Public vs Private Sector Myths* (New York: PublicAffairs, 2013).

3. Jonathan Gruber and Simon Johnson, *Jump-Starting America: How Breakthrough Science Can Revive Economic Growth and the American Dream* (New York: Hachette Book Group, 2019).

4. Gruber and Johnson, *Jump-Starting America*.

5. Orin Hoffman, Laura Manley, Michael Kearney, Amritha Jayanti, Tess Cushing, and Raina Gandhi, "Building a 21st-Century American Economy," The Role of Tough Tech in Ensuring Shared, Sustainable Prosperity," Harvard Kennedy School, Belfer Center, November 2020, https://www.belfercenter.org/publication/building -21st-century-american-economy.

6. Fred L. Block and Matthew R. Keller, *State of Innovation: the US Government's Role in Technology Development* (New York: Routledge, 2011).

7. Daniel Traficonte, "Patents over Planning: Industrial Capital and Federal Innovation Policy," PhD diss., Massachusetts Institute of Technology, 2021.

8. Brian Lucking, Nicholas Bloom, and John Van Reenen, "Have R&D Spillovers Declined in the 21st Century?," *Fiscal Studies* 40, no. 4 (2019): 561–590.

9. This section draws from multiple perspectives on this topic. See Erik Brynjolfsson, Seth Benzell, and Daniel Rock, "Understanding and Addressing the Modern Productivity Paradox," MIT Work of the Future Research Brief 13-2020, November 10, 2020; John Van Reenen, "Innovation Policies to Boost Productivity," Policy Proposal, The Hamilton Project, June 2020, https://www.hamiltonproject.org/assets/files/JVR_PP _LO_6.15_FINAL.pdf; Nicholas Bloom, John Van Reenen, and Heidi Williams, "A Toolkit of Policies to Promote Innovation," *Journal of Economic Perspectives* 33, no. 3 (August 2019): 163–184; and Gruber and Johnson, *Jump-Starting America*.

10. See Pierre Azoulay, Joshua S. Graff Zivin, Danielle Li, and Bhaven N. Sampat, "Public R&D Investments and Private-Sector Patenting: Evidence from NIH Funding Rules," *Review of Economic Studies* 86, no. 1 (January 2019): 117–152. This research shows that public R&D investments made by the National Institutes of Health translate into substantial increases in private sector patenting.

11. Robert M. Solow, "Technical Change and the Aggregate Production Function," *Review of Economics and Statistics* 39, no. 3 (August 1957): 312–320.

12. Hoffman et al., "Building a 21st-Century American Economy."

13. Van Reenen, "Innovation Policies to Boost Productivity."

14. Yasheng Huang and Meicen Sun, "China's Development in Artificial Intelligence," MIT Work of the Future Research Brief, 2021.

15. Van Reenen, "Innovation Policies to Boost Productivity."

16. See Hoffman et al., "Building a 21st-Century American Economy."

17. Elisabeth B. Reynolds, Hiram M. Samel, and Joyce Lawrence, "Learning by Building: Complementary Assets and the Migration of Capabilities in U.S. Innovation Firms," in *Production in the Innovation Economy,* ed. Richard M. Locke and Rachel L. Wellhausen (Cambridge, MA: MIT Press, 2014).

18. See Mercedes Delgado and Karen G. Mills, "The Supply Chain Economy: A New Industry Categorization for Understanding Innovation in Services," *Research Policy* 49, no. 8 (2020), art. 104039; and Mercedes Delgado and Karen G. Mills, "The

Supply Chain Economy: A New Industry Categorization for Understanding Innovation in Services," *Research Policy* 49, no. 8 (2020): 104039.

19. Benjamin Armstrong, "A Firm-level Study of Workforce Challenges at US Manufacturers," MIT Work of the Future Working Paper No. 12, 2021.

20. For an analysis of regional trends and of strategies to address regional decline, see Ryan Nunn and Jay Shambaugh, "The Geography of Prosperity," Brookings Institution, September 2018, https://www.brookings.edu/research/the-geography-of-prosperity; and Clara Hendrickson, Mark Muro, and William A. Galston, "Strategies for Left-Behind Places," and Benjamin Austin, Edward Glaeser, and Lawrence Summers, "Jobs for the Heartland: Place-Based Policies in 21st Century America," both in *Brookings Papers on Economic Activity*, Spring 2018.

21. See Robert D. Atkinson, Mark Muro, and Jacob Whiton, "The Case for Growth Centers: How to Spread Tech Innovation across America," Brookings Institution, December 19, 2019. https://www.brookings.edu/research/growth-centers-how-to-spread-tech-innovation-across-america.

22. Gruber and Johnson, *Jump-Starting America*.

23. Daron Acemoglu, Andrea Manera and Pascual Restrepo, "Taxes, Automation, and the Future of Labor," MIT Work of the Future Research Brief, 2020.

24. Economics teaches us that regardless of who nominally pays the tax (firm or worker), its incidence falls partly on both. Regardless of whether the tax ultimately reduces wages or reduces profits, however, it creates an economic wedge between pay and productivity, which distorts investment away from labor and toward capital, where the wedge is smaller.

25. Daron Acemoglu and Pascual Restrepo, "The Race between Man and Machine: Implications of Technology for Growth, Factor Shares, and Employment," *American Economic Review* 108, no. 6 (2018): 1488–1542.

26. Matthew Smith, Danny Yagan, Owen Zidar, and Eric Zwick, "Capitalists in the Twenty-First Century," *Quarterly Journal of Economics* 134, no. 4 (2019): 1675–1745.

27. Acemoglu, Manera, and Restrepo, "Taxes, Automation, and the Future of Labor."

28. Nicholas Bloom, John Van Reenen, and Heidi Williams, "A Toolkit of Policies to Promote Innovation," *Journal of Economic Perspectives* 33, no. 3 (August 2019): 163–184.

MIT TASK FORCE ON THE WORK OF THE FUTURE RESEARCH BRIEFS

<hr>

MIT TASK FORCE ON THE WORK OF THE FUTURE

David Autor, Co-Chair, Department of Economics

David A. Mindell, Co-Chair, Department of Aeronautics and Astronautics; Program in Science, Technology, and Society; Founder and Executive Chairman, Humatics Corporation

Elisabeth B. Reynolds, Former Executive Director, MIT Industrial Performance Center; Special Assistant to the President, Manufacturing and Economic Development, National Economic Council

TASK FORCE MEMBERS

Suzanne Berger, Department of Political Science

Erik Brynjolfsson, Stanford Digital Economy Lab

John Gabrieli, Department of Brain and Cognitive Sciences

John Hart, Department of Mechanical Engineering

Yasheng Huang, Sloan School of Management

Jason Jackson, Department of Urban Studies and Planning

Thomas Kochan, Sloan School of Management

John Leonard, Department of Mechanical Engineering

Paul Osterman, Sloan School of Management

Iyad Rahwan, MIT Media Lab

Daniela Rus, Department of Electrical Engineering and Computer Science

Sanjay Sarma, Department of Mechanical Engineering
Julie Shah, Department of Aeronautics and Astronautics
Tavneet Suri, Sloan School of Management
Kathleen Thelen, Department of Political Science
John Van Reenen, Sloan School of Management
Krystyn Van Vliet, Department of Materials Science and Engineering
Christine Walley, Department of Anthropology

TASK FORCE ADVISORY BOARD

Roger C. Altman, Founder & Senior Chairman, Evercore
Ana Botin, Executive Chairman, Santander Group
Charlie Braun, President, Custom Rubber Corp.
Eric Cantor, Vice Chairman, Moelis & Company
Volkmar Denner, Chairman of the Board, Robert Bosch GMBH
William Clay Ford, Jr., Executive Chairman, Ford Motor Company
Jennifer Granholm, US Secretary of Energy; Former Governor of Michigan
Freeman A. Hrabowski, III, President, University of Maryland, Baltimore
    County
David H. Long, Chairman and CEO, Liberty Mutual Insurance
Karen Mills, Senior Fellow, Harvard Business School
Indra Nooyi, Former Chairman and CEO, PepsiCo
Annette Parker, President, South Central College, Minnesota
David Rolf, Founder and President Emeritus, SEIU 775
Ginni M. Rometty, Former Chairman, President, and CEO, IBM
Juan Salgado, Chancellor, City Colleges of Chicago
Eric E. Schmidt, Technical Advisor and Member of the Board, Alphabet,
    Inc.
Elizabeth Shuler, Secretary-Treasurer, AFL-CIO
David M. Siegel, Co-Chairman, Two Sigma
Robert Solow, Professor Emeritus, MIT Economics
Darren Walker, President, Ford Foundation
Jeff Wilke, Chairman, Re:Build Manufacturing
Marjorie Yang, Chairman, Esquel Group

TASK FORCE RESEARCH ADVISORY BOARD MEMBERS

William Bonvillian, Lecturer, MIT

Rodney Brooks, Professor Emeritus, MIT; Founder and CTO Robust.ai

Joshua Cohen, Distinguished Senior Fellow in Law, Philosophy, and Political Science, University of California, Berkeley

Virginia Dignum, Professor of Social & Ethical AI, Umeå University

Susan Helper, Professor, Case Western Reserve University

Susan Houseman, Vice President and Director of Research, W. E. Upjohn Institute

John Irons, Senior Vice President and Head of Research, Siegel Family Endowment

Martin Krzywdzinski, Principal Investigator, WZB Berlin Social Science Center

Frank Levy, Rose Professor Emeritus, MIT

Fei-Fei Li, Professor, Computer Science Department, Stanford University

Nichola J. Lowe, Professor, Department of City and Regional Planning, University of North Carolina, Chapel Hill

Joel Mokyr, Professor of Economics and History, Northwestern University

Michael Piore, David W. Skinner Professor of Political Economy, Emeritus, MIT Department of Economics

Gill Pratt, CEO, Toyota Research Institute

INDEX

Wages (cont.)
  and sector-based training, 83–84, 88
  and shareholder capitalism, 111–112
  and union membership, 115
  and upward mobility, 32–33
  wage comparisons, 26, 101, 119
  and worker education, 20–21, 92
Wagner Act of 1935, 37
Wagner-Peyser Act of 1933, 95
Walley, Christine, 38
Walmart, 111–112, 116
Warehouses, automated, 43, 58–64
  digital job boards, 61
  picking and packing, 60, 62
  and robotics, 62–63
  shipping self-service, 61–62
  truck brokerage and scheduling, 61
  warehouse management systems, 62
Watson system, 44
Weil, David, 38
West Point, 121–122
Westward expansion, 122
Whole-of-government approach, 127
Wisconsin Regional Training Partner-
    ship, 83
Women's wages, 19
Work
  digitalization of, 16, 23–24
  as human good, 9
  new occupations, 13–15
Worker compensation. *See* Wages
Workers. *See also* Low-wage workers
  African American, 19, 27–29, 115–116
  agricultural/domestic, 103, 115–117,
    139
  dislocated, 40, 92–93, 137
  gig, 38, 119
  health care, 49, 110
  high-wage, 19–23, 27
  Hispanic, 19, 27–28
  hospitality, 116
  as stakeholders, 111–119

Workforce Innovation and Opportunity
    Act (WIOA) of 2014, 85, 92, 94–95
Workforce Investment Act, 94
Working Washington, 118
Wraparound support, 85
Wright Brothers, 42

Year Up, 83, 96
YouTube, 99

Zoox, 54